CHRISTIAN DEVELOPMENT AND MATURATION

REVD. M.S. JOHNSON

Order this book online at www.trafford.com
or email orders@trafford.com

Most Trafford titles are also available at major online book retailers.

Printed in Victoria, BC, Canada.

ISBN: 978-1-4120-9830-4

*Our mission is to efficiently provide the world's finest, most comprehensive book publishing
service, enabling every author to experience success. To find out how to publish your book, your
way, and have it available worldwide, visit us online at www.trafford.com*

Trafford rev. 11/19/2009

 www.trafford.com

North America & international
toll-free: 1 888 232 4444 (USA & Canada)
phone: 250 383 6864 ♦ fax: 812 355 4082

DEDICATION

I dedicate this book to the memory of my beloved mother Sylvena Russell, whose consistent saintly Christian living and her prayers for my conversion lead me to accept Jesus as my Saviour, many years before she died in 1989 at the age of 88.

I also include my youngest sister Gladys May Russell in this dedication in memory of her life and work as a dear servant of God at home, as well as her work at Up Park Camp in the military corp. In additional to serving her country and people as Secretary to several Chiefs of Staff in the Jamaica Defence Force, she also served as secretary to her local church in August Town, Kingston, Jamaica. Gladys died on the 30th August 2005 at the age of 67.

This book is dedicated to mother and daughter. They both shared the blessings of God together and have touched the lives of people, not only in Jamaica but around the world and they certainly

DEDICATION

touched my life.They hold onto me in memory and their souls rest in peace.

CHRISTIAN DEVELOPMENT AND MATURATION

PREFACE

During the past forty-five years, I have had a very strong urge to write a book about the different stages of Christian development and maturation, but that was as far as it went.

Recently I met one of my ministerial colleagues who it seems, God used to motivate me to fulfil my ambition. This preface will hopefully be of benefit to anyone who like myself wants to share their experience with others.

Christianity is a personal involvement in matters of the church at various levels, and about spiritual problems. I likened this to a university, which teaches several different subjects of different faculties.

Christianity in many ways is similar to the birth and growth of a child. After the birth of the child, the parents, especially the mother, must spend quality time day and night nurturing and training the infant. In order that he or she may reach the age when they can manage on their own, and come to maturity. He or she will be able to accumulate their own experiences to go through the rest of their life on earth.

Nicodemus did not understand when Jesus told him that he must be born again in order to see the kingdom of God. He could not understand what being born-again meant, as this was the first time anyone on earth had ever heard that saying.

The writer of the book of Hebrews in chapter eleven and verse one declares that *'faith is the substance of things hoped for and the evidence of things not seen'*. This means that one must first believe in the Bible and obey its doctrine in order to receive the reward and blessings that faith in God affords.

The Bible also says that obedience is the recipe to long life. Christian obedience is therefore one of the attitudes a young Christian must embrace, like a young child, if it must learn from its parent the basic principles of life.

There are several objects of worship that the people of the world pray to, and in doing so, fervently believe that their object of worship hears them when they pray and answers their prayers. Prayer is therefore a powerful medium of spiritual communication, which Jesus personally did and recommended as man's only way of approach to God. Faith and prayer are two of the most powerful weapons available to the believer in his search for God. The Bible contains many instances of positive

CHRISTIAN DEVELOPMENT AND MATURATION

prayers and faith, which divides great bodies of water, cause the cessation of drought, and brought back the dead to life and more.

Like nutrients to the natural body, so are spiritual virtues to the spiritual body. One of the nine fruits of the spirit is love, and Jesus gave a very apt parable to his disciples on love for God and ones neighbour; *'love God with all of your heart, soul and mind, and your neighbour as yourself'*. None of the ten commandments of the Old Testament is greater than that kind of love.

The gospel is the good news from heaven, brought to earth by Jesus Christ. He gave it to his disciples in parables free of cost. The gospel, was meant to prepare men for the kingdom of heaven, throughout his relatively short life on earth Jesus taught his disciples the heart of Christian worship and skills in telling the good news to those who have not heard it; even in the uttermost parts of the earth, he promised to be with them wherever they went spreading the gospel.

The man who was born blind refused to be silenced by the critics of Jesus and his disciples, even when told to be quiet about the healing of his blind eyes. When one has proven that the product is good and he wants others to have it too, he will make every effort to sell it to anyone who wants it.

Jesus declares in one of the gospels that he was greater than Moses, Solomon and all of the great patriarchs of the Old Testament. His greatness and leadership was revolutionary and unique, it had to be; because he was setting the stage for the coming of the world's cure for the oldest disease, sin.

Of all the disciples who believed on Jesus and followed him for some time, he chose only twelve, one of whom was a traitor. He commissioned the twelve to preach the gospel to every corner of the earth, and in doing so, to be fearless leaders even unto death. A courageous Christian leader is therefore an attractive and high occupation, not by secular professional standards, because it offers very little material incentives. His ultimate rewards will be worth the sacrifices he makes. A Christian leader is therefore not a hireling, but a specially chosen instrument of God's service on earth, and given divine courage and ability to do his duty as a faithful servant of Christ. The task he or she faces constantly are not just human, they are Satan-motivated, deadly and except for Jesus' promises to be with his disciples to the end of the age, we could not survive.

For an aeroplane to take off and become airborne it must have the power to take off, not just to speed down the runway and stop at the end of it.

The motor vehicle, regardless of its external beauty, must have an engine under the bonnet that can fire the pistons in order to gather momentum and thrust to move from point A to point B. If the engine is not designed with a fuel tank and system to pump the fuel to the various components, which together cause the engine to fire, it is not serving its purpose. They would therefore have to push it, but it was not made to push and pull.

The Christian believers are types of engines with abilities, potentials and drive, but those same individuals with their abilities, skills and drive is not enough to perform, except he or she is fitted with a clean adequate and appropriate system to contain the Holy Spirit.

Having all the appropriate human propensities that only the social elites are privileged or accustom to having, these are only material possession as required by the social status-quo, the spiritual status-quo is a gift from God which only they who are worthy can have.

Spiritual worthiness is not allotted to the social elites in high society; it comes from the spiritual relationship that exist in God, which is the reason why the local church in a community does not seem to always attract the majority of the local inhabitants to its activities as it should. People believe what they see and hear. If we as Christians fail to make plain to the non-Christian what we are portraying to them, or if we give the wrong signal, we will be like a man trying to catch fish from a river, and instead of the right bait he throws stones which only frighten

PREFACE

the fishes away.

This brings me to the end of my brief comments of what this book intends to highlight in the following chapters.

INTRODUCTION

I was born in the Caribbean island of Jamaica on the 7th March 1920 in the district of Mulletthall. This is not far from the town of Chapelton in the parish of Clarendon where my parents lived. Later we moved to Main Ridge where I went to school at the age of 7, and later still we moved down to Cocoa Walk at the western side of Chapelton. There I continued my schooling from the age of 10 at Kellits Elementary School at Woodhall, I finally finished schooling in 1936.

Having reached standard six and not being able to continue into secondary education, I went into agricultural farming until 1944. During the Second World War I travelled to Kingston in search of a better job and was fortunate to find employment at the Belmont Dry Docks, where I worked as an apprentice painter and this was my first experience of working away from home and earning a wage packet. This was my greatest joy, my first pay packet of 25 shillings which was increased to 30 shillings

6 months later. In less than 9 months I was a fully trained painter, able to paint both boats and houses. I remained in that employment until I migrated to the UK in October 1959.

On New Years day 1956, I was converted to the Christian faith and was baptised three months later. After that I took up fellowship at the Franklin Town Church of God at 16 Albert Street, Kingston, Jamaica. Then in October 1959 I travelled to the UK in search of better living conditions and better wages, but surprisingly I earned less than one might have expected, being askilled worker in Jamaica, my wages in Jamaica were more than I was able to earn in the UK after all the deductions were made. However, these were only social and economic matters: the greater stages of my life were yet to come, the spiritual part of my life.

Arriving in the UK as a Christian, finding the right place or church to worship was not that easy. Most of our choices of places to worship were Pentecostal and Black-led churches and there were no such groups or churches anywhere in the areas where we lived. Nevertheless, where I had lived and worked in Kingston, Jamaica, I was accustomed to meeting with all classes and races and therefore I refused to be put off from worshipping God on the grounds that I couldn't find a church group of my liking. So I went out to find a place of worship and I found a Baptist church in Corsham, Wiltshire, on the street near to where I was staying at 69 Priory Street. After visiting that church for a few weeks and finding new friends there, I later moved to the Brethren Assembly on Station Road, Corsham. I continued there until the time came when I was invited to preach the word of God at other churches.

Following this were several similar invitations from various churches in and around the towns of Corsham, Chippenham, Christian Malford, Lacock and as far as Warminster, inviting me to preach at their meetings. However my chief place of worship at that time was the Brethren Assembly at Station Road, Corsham. Then in 1964 I was invited to join a newly formed New Testament Church of God at the Liberal Hall, Chippenham. I was with that church until we later bought the old St Peter's church at Lowden, Chippenham; the Pastor then was Rev S.C. Wright.

Whilst at St Peter's I was invited to sit the examination for the ministry, which I did and passed at the same time I continued preaching in Chippenham as well as at other churches in and around Chippenham. From there I was later appointed District Youth and Christian Education Director for the Gloucester District of the New Testament Church of God. The District of Gloucester then included Gloucester, Bristol, Bath, Wiltshire and South Wales. I held this office until 1969 when I was appointed Pastor of the New Testament Church of God in Trowbridge. Within the time of my pastorate I have pastored at two churches in England and one in Jamaica. I have been Exhorter, Licensed and Ordained Minister, but more importantly I have been a servant of God preaching and teaching the gospel of the Lord Jesus Christ.

I retired from Pastoral Ministry in 1996, but not from preaching and teaching which I intend to do until my death, God being my helper.

Chapter 1

─────────

CHRISTIAN CONVERSION

A Christian is one who has accepted Christ as Saviour having been born again into the body of Christ by conversion. The transition is not popular or natural to the way of thinking or understanding of man. Nicodemus went to hold a conversation with Jesus, believing that Jesus was a teacher from God due to the miracles that he had seen him perform. But Jesus, who knows all things without anyone having to tell him, went straight to the core of what Nicodemus needed to know. Jesus told him that he had to be born again, *John 3:1-7.* This is similar to Christian conversion, where as in natural childbirth a child is born following a relationship between a man and a woman, a similar relationship is true between a sinner and his/her saviour. It doesn't matter how old or how young you are, what nationality or physical attributes you have, or economic or social status. The transition to new birth remains the same, *Romans 10:9-13.* You must believe in your heart and confess with your mouth that you believe in the death and resurrection of Jesus Christ, and that you accept him as Lord of your life in order to experience the new birth.

To be born again is truly a miracle, that a person could live a sinful life for almost all the days of his or her life and then suddenly become conscious of wrong doings. What would come to their mind is *John 1:8-9* 'If we say that we have no sin we deceive ourselves and the truth is not in us. But if we confess our sins, he is faithful and just to forgive our sins and to cleanse us from all unrighteousness'. One may say at this point 'I am a sinner and I don't always read my bible, how is it possible that these verses of scripture could enter my mind?' My answer would be that as soon as consciousness of wrong-doing (sin) comes to one's mind, the presence of the Holy Spirit is at hand. Conviction of your sin will therefore follow, leading you to repentance.

It is to this end that Jesus promised his disciples in *John 14:16,26,* if you read these scriptures you will see for yourself that God is always ahead of us with ideas and information to guide us and deliver us out of all our difficult situations. All we need to do is to be willing to obey and follow the directions that the Holy Spirit brings to our attention.

This then takes me to the point that I made earlier, to be born again or conversion is a miracle. The fact

CHRISTIAN DEVELOPMENT AND MATURATION

is that however long you have lived in sin or however bad your sinful deeds have been, within seconds of confessing and repenting of those sins, God in his merciful forgiveness and compassion will remove your sin. He will place you in a situation such as if you had never done anything wrong throughout your life. To me this is one of the greatest miracles that have ever taken place and I am glad that it affects my life as well. Praise God.

However, being born into the family of Christ involves a process of growth, which is as natural and normal as any healthy birth. The first stage of the new birth entails the word of the gospel being delivered in various ways, whether we hear it from a pulpit, through a gospel tract, the TV, radio or on the street corner, *Mark 16:15-16 records that Jesus gave his followers* a commission to take the gospel to all nations. The first clause of *verse 16* reads 'he that believes and is baptised shall be saved'. This tells me that Christian believers should be baptised. *Verse 17-18* describes another stage in the believer's process of growth, signs that follow believers. My understanding of this is that the believers with whom these signs are identified are those who stand on the promises of the Lord. They make every effort to avail themselves to be used by God and to accomplish his glory.

In my personal experience as a minister of the gospel and as a Pastor of congregations for many years, I have seen that there are not many believers in the Christian church who actively show any real effort or interest towards spiritual attainment, other than praise and worship.

Another stage in the process of growth of the believer is that of sanctification. *1 Corinthians 1:2* refers to them that are sanctified in Christ Jesus, called to be saints, with all that in every place called upon the name of Jesus Christ our Lord. He is to all of us Lord and Saviour. *1 Corinthians 6:9-10* reminds the Christian believers of the conditions of sins that we are forgiven. *Verse 11* states '*and such were some of us, but we are washed, we are sanctified and we are made justified because of what God has done for us through Jesus and the Holy Spirit*'. The sanctified believer being set apart from sins, we have an obligation to live holy lives to please God who called us out of the darkness of sin into his marvellous light of salvation.

Paul as the spiritual father of his flock prayed in *1 Thessalonians 5:23-24*, that the God of peace may sanctify their lives completely and that they may be totally preserved through the spirit until the coming of the Lord. Paul knew full well that it was only possible for the believer, once set free and forgiven from sin, could only remain saved through sanctification. They would have to continue to serve the Lord in obedience and humbleness of mind, spirit and soul. These are the stages that Christian believers must pursue on their way to maturity.

Unfortunately some believers do not seem to care whether or not they need to do anything more than say their prayers, read their bibles and go to church meetings whenever it is possible. They say God knows their intentions; he knows that they mean well and that they love their brothers, sisters and other family members. They don't steal or use swear words nor smoke and are not fornicators or adulterers. They are as good as any other Christians and no one is perfect so why try to be what you cannot be? God knows my heart and that's what matters.

However just as in life a man or woman naturally progresses into maturity, so the spiritual process of development also continues as long as life lasts. And with maturity comes a certain amount of privileges, which are also available to family members who can share in the family fortune.

I referred earlier to *Mark 16:16-18* on the subject of what is believed, and as explained then, the whole Christian development moves through the stages as a continual programme. The first is entry into salvation according to the above text. Those who believe and are baptised are saved whereas those who do not believe shall be condemned (pronounced unfit).

Those of us who are converted into the Pentecostal Christian faith are well acquainted with the customs followed after conversion, baptism, and acceptance into fellowship etc. This is all part of what we believe but no one forces you into doing what you do not believe.

Mark 16:17 Jesus said '*These signs shall follow them that believe; in my name they shall cast out demons, they shall speak with new tongues*'. The whole concept depends on what you believe i.e. the expression or idea. If you believe a thing to be of interest to you, you are likely to go after it. It is not all family members who will show interest in the family's fortune especially if they have to make contribution, or work hard to pay towards producing something.

Mark 16:18 talks of taking up serpents, but who wants to pick up a snake you may ask? But it could be that the snakes that comes in your path at times are unavoidable and to be able to put them under control or get rid of them could be of great help to those affected by them. Also, they shall lay hands on the sick and they shall recover, and if they themselves drink any poisonous thing they will recover. This might never happen in a lifetime, but in case it does we would be glad not to be killed by it. Most of us Christians or our families and friends suffered various illness, wouldn't we be glad to have someone in our church fellowship, who when they laid hands on any sick person, they can be healed, especially when doctors cannot help?

As I write this, it is the first day of the year 2006.

And the prayer of my heart is that God will help us as a body of people in the Church of God, not only my local fellowship in Trowbridge, Wiltshire but throughout Britain and around the world; that we will earnestly contend for the faith, with all that it takes to believe in God enough to see these promises come true to us as a church, before the end of 2006 and ultimately before I die. I pray this in Jesus name, Amen.

The Promise of *Mark 16:17-18*. When one begins to develop a passion for the promises of God as mentioned in the scriptures, the Spirit of God is at hand to remind us of where in the word of God these promises are to be found. For example *Eph 4:11-16* and *1 Cor 12:4-31,* and also chapter 13 are valuable for counselling. Of course when one reads these promises of God in the scriptures, with a desire in mind to please God, you will find that the more you read God's words of promise the more the Holy Spirit reveals the wisdom of God's word to you, there are words of truth and grace through sufficient scriptures for all those who have a passion for work and service, available to those that love God and their fellowman. Here the words of a song comes to mind:-

'I will do my part'
(1) It may be little that I can do, nor may I have much to say, But in that little I mean to be true,

and to do what I can today. (Chorus)
(2) The work he giveth may lowly be, it may not win man's applause, but if I do what he chooses of me, I know it will help his cause. (Chorus)
(3) In vain no service that love may give, no matter how small it be, in God's remembrance it ever shall live, to shine in eternity. (Chorus)
(4) In that fair day when the crowns are bought for those who have faithful proved, there will be one for each soul that has wrought, for all that have worked and lived. (Chorus)
Chorus
From the depths of my heart I will do my part,
With a ready and willing hand,
And I will not shirk I will faithfully work,
In the place that my Lord has planned.

The words of this song have been a source inspiration throughout the 50 years of my walk with the Lord, and I hope it will be as long as I live. The words offer a challenge to any Christian who wants to develop into maturity. Like a young adolescent starting out in his or her first experience of work, doing the job he or she chooses to do to earn a livelihood. Their aim is to be highly qualified so that they can earn a good salary to buy the things they need most. Likewise when a young Christian reads words like, *"Behold I will send you the promise of*

CHRISTIAN DEVELOPMENT AND MATURATION

the Father, but wait until the Holy Spirit fills you with power, Luke 24:49, (speaking of the ability to serve), or *Acts 1:8* says *"that you will receive power when the Holy Spirit comes on you. Then you will be able to be witness onto me wherever you go".*

If you are a Christian with a strong desire to do something big for God's glory, you receive promises like these and believe them to be true as it is the Bible that says so and you believe the Bible to be God's word, that depth of belief in a God that does not lie and cannot fail will undoubtedly make you willing and obedient to do all that the word of God tells you to do. This is so in order to make you a successful follower of God, especially as it is recorded in the scriptures, how God has used ordinary men and women, like you and me, to do extra-ordinary things. This was so in those times but the scriptures also say the same can happen in our present modern-day lives. Jesus who gave men and women power through the Holy Spirit and through signs and miracles that they did in their days, is the same Jesus using men and women today.

As I penned these words the Holy Spirit revealed to me that all we need to do is to earnestly contend for the faith that was once given to the saints. (Please read *Jude verse 2 and verses 20 -21)* also, if you read these words of Jude who was the half brother of our Lord Jesus Christ, and believe in your heart that they are God's word, I know that it will make a difference to your whole spiritual life. Praise God.

It is my intention to exhort my readers in another chapter of this book, that Christians should make every possible effort to build a spiritual relationship with Jesus Christ and the Holy Spirit. They should by reading the Bible, and by constant prayer, ask God to speak to their hearts through the Holy Spirit, so that they may be directed by the Word of God towards all truths, they need to know to make them a true followers of God all the remaining days of their life.

My friends less than your best for Christ is not worth living, you also owe it to yourself to be the best you can be and no one else can do you that favour. Many of us still try to help others to be their best in Christ, because we have lived to see and enjoy the blessings of God all because we tried to do our best in Christ. And it paid off to the extent that God has used us to be a blessing to others, so now we in turn are exhorting others to share in our blessings and bless others by sharing your stories of how God blesses you. That in itself is spiritual maturation developing within you, God bless you.

Chapter 2

CHRISTIAN OBEDIENCE

In chapter one I tentatively mentioned obedience; I am now going to elaborate upon what I said then and what is meant in the literal as well as in the spiritual sense. In order for me to generate knowledge about the word obedience as far as God's concern, I must take you back to Adam and Eve in the Garden of Eden.

As far as can be imagined, they had their first meeting with God and every thing was as perfect as the world which God made, and the paradise he prepared for them and placed them in. Their duty was simply to obey what God had said and the terms and conditions under which they were to occupy the garden. The responsibility was not on Eve but on Adam, it was absolutely important for him to understand all that God told him at this early stage and what his responsibilities thereafter would be, because if he did not obey what God had said, the entire plan of God would be disrupted before it started. God made man to help in replenishing the earth but where man fails, God's plan fails also because God in his divine plan was depending on man's obedience and faithfulness to see his plan through.

Adam was shown all of the fruit-bearing trees in the garden and the fruits that they bear, the tree of knowledge of good and evil was also specially pointed out to him and the consequences that would follow if he should take and eat its fruit. Obedience to God's words at this initial stage was the only obligation Adam had to observe, he was free to do whatsoever else he wants, it was he who named all the animals, the birds, the fishes that swam in all the waters, the trees and everything else that God made on earth. It was he who named all the birds that flew in the air, he had power and authority.

At this stage of creation Adam had no choice, and from a human point of view, he did not need to have a choice, if he did God would have given him one or several. God gave Adam and his partner all they needed to live in comfort, all he wanted them to do was to obey him. In spite of all this freedom, God gave them the capacity to develop and exercise a will and the power of choice. The bible says that God gave Adam the appropriate helper that was necessary for him, that helper was Eve.

Adam was focused and this was how God wanted it to be. He was the first human being that God made. God also wanted the first man he made to recognise him for whom he is, Satan knew this all along, so he wanted man to loose the connection he had with his maker. He also knew the blessings that God had in store for him, but he could not go through the man and that Eve was the soft target and the more vulnerable of the two so he went directly for her. He said to her "God knows that you would be as wise as him, knowing good and evil, that is why he told Adam not to eat of the fruits from the tree of knowledge of good and evil".

From the creation of the first man until now, his existence depends on God. Man's willingness to obey and to respond to his divine will was not in question until man began to think and act as if he was as wise as God. However, this does not mean that he is as wise as God or ever can, he was made to serve and serve he must. God could have compel Adam to render without fail the type of service he wanted him to provide, but that would be the sort of service a robot provides for its maker, but God does not need the services of robots, he requires willingness from us. Even the angels have freedom of worship, if this was not so, Lucifer could not have rebelled, because of this rebellion, he and his followers were put out of Heaven by force.

To rectify the situation caused by the rebellion of Satan, Jesus avail himself and was willing to come to earth ruined by Satan to redeem man from his lost estate. It took God himself to provide that condescending willingness; a mystery we will never understand as long as we remain finite, and clothed himself in sinfulness for to show his unimaginable love for lost man. Having his love as a model of all love, we must also be willing to shower our world with the same kind of love that is shed abroad in our hearts. Jesus volunteered his love to us, not because we were good but because of the potential he sees in man. When people volunteer to do something, they do so hoping to get some satisfaction and pleasure. The potential Jesus saw in us we will never know, but the bible says that he shall see the travail of his soul and be satisfied, *Isaiah 53:10 - 11.* When we serve God in spite of the dangers attached, if we are willing it will be easier. This type of willingness is reflected in the words of this song:-

> *"There was one who was willing to die in my stead,*
> *That soul so unworthy might live and the path to the cross he*
> *Was willing to tread,*
> *All the sins of my life to forgive,'*

This stanza is a fitting tribute to Jesus for the willingness he showed when he died for us. But his death was not an ordinary one; he suffered excruciating pain in order to show his divine love for humanity, who he had to retrieve from the curse of sin brought on the entire human race because of Adams transgression.

Unfortunately for Adam, he did not realize the elaborate preparation God made for their future and the future of all mankind, the book of Genesis said that the paradise they were in before they disobeyed God and were expelled from the garden was perpetual freedom. They were absolutely free to do what they like in a sinless, painless and death-free environment, but all that ceased after they were turned out of the garden, and had to toil and sweat for their existence, which was not, what God planned for them.

All that changed after Satan introduced himself to Eve as her adviser. Eve never met Satan before and Adam never mentioned him to her, because he also never met him nor knew anything about him and nothing was said to Adam by God. But now the whole of man's future depended on the reply Eve was going to give Satan's question. *"Did God say you should not eat of every tree of the garden?"* We now know what her answer was and the consequences it brought to the human race. All of the pain and suffering of nations brought on by war and strife, all of the hunger and hardship, the evil and eventual death, happened as a result of the meeting between Satan and Eve. This woeful meeting opened a brand new sphere of communication. Her eyes were indeed opened, and she was now in a position to realise good and evil and exercise her power of choice, which she did not know how to evaluate at the time.

Satan's response as far as Eve was concerned was so profound that she had to introduce the concept to Adam who did not question what his wife told him; instead he gladly indulged and became co-partner in the deception. All kinds of suffering and sorrow emerged from Satan's deception of the first two people God put on earth, but God also had his plan, and his plan for man's redemption in the advent of Jesus, ready to destroy the works of the devil.

Although they may not have known then the paradise which they enjoyed, before they knew they had a choice, but to make things worse, they made the wrong choice, when they disobeyed God and were expelled from the garden. They had lost fellowship, everlasting life, everlasting happiness, freedom and the close fellowship they had in the presence of God.

Having lost fellowship with God by disobedience, and disobedience is sin, man had to be removed from the presence of God because sin separates man from God. Adam had no appropriate offering to God for his transgression because there was none available to him at that time, the only thing they could do was to offer excuses. Adam blamed the woman God gave him, the woman blamed the serpent but the serpent did not offer any.

Disobedience is therefore the cause of man's past and present predicament. This predicament will continue until the return of Jesus Christ to establish his new kingdom on earth, this time a kingdom that is infallible. He is God's ransom for sin and transgression, so there is no need to find an excuse.

Obedience and faith in God are the two paramount parallels that God requires from all who decide to follow him, from the heart in pursuit of his grace, mercy and material blessing that was promised to Abraham and his seed.

This blessing is conditional; to receive it one must possess and practice the faith and obedience, which was found in Abraham and his seed after him. This faith and obedience in the almighty, was that which prompted Noah to move with fear and build the ark according to God's specification, that rescue a specimen of the human race, which would have been lost otherwise.

Those rescued by the ark was pronounced righteous by God himself, in spite of the state the world is in now, but it was from that remnant the present world population of over six billion originated. This is hard evidence of the positive result of faith And obedience to God's work. Faith and obedience takes prominence over other virtues. It was the reason behind Noah's undertaking to build the ark, so faith and work co-exist, both work together because although Noah had faith, that alone could not complete the task God placed in his care, he had to put his faith into action in order to achieve what he did; and we know that it was because of his faith and work that saved the earth and it's population from destruction and God's eternal judgement.

At present we are living in a very dangerous stage of human existence, it is a time when God is about to visit the earth again like he did during Noah's time. God may be calling you because he sees that he can rely on you to obey him, and do exactly as he said. In doing what God wants you to do, may mean offending some people, however, if you are sure it is the voice of God you hear speaking to you, do whatsoever he says. Make a move, perhaps by doing so, some may be saved before it is too late.

Another powerful example of obedience was Abraham. He was called by God to go on a journey he knew nothing about, but he trusted God, if you are going to be a type of messenger God wants, you must trust him to prove his faithfulness in fulfilling his word. What we know about Abraham is that he trusted God to lead him, knowing that he would lead him right.

By disobedience God's original plan for man became dormant for a while, since then God is gradually unfolding the content and detail of a new plan. That new plan and its foundation laid somewhere between Iraq and Iran, the birthplace of Abraham thousands of years ago. Although Abraham's father Terah was a professional maker and worshipper of idols, God chose that family to be the progenitor of the Jewish nation from which Jesus the Messiah of that nation and saviour of the world came.

This was an indication that God wanted to re-establish a working relationship with falling man, a relationship that must be establish on a criteria similar to that on which the first Adam was established, obedience.

The following is the Bible's statement of God's call to Abraham: "*Now the Lord had said unto Abraham, get thee out of thy country and from thy kindred and from thy fathers house, unto a land that I will show thee; and I will make thee a great nation, and I will bless thee and make thy name great; thou shalt be a blessing*". *Gen 12: 1-2.*

The bible also says "*Abraham believed in the Lord; and he counted it to him for righteousness.*" *Gen 15:6*

Obedience is a positive response to an instruction. The call on Abraham was not a dream, it was the real voice of the real God, telling him to leave his fathers house and his kindred, and he did not tell him where he would be going. Abraham had his faith and faith will always find a way.

After Abraham heard the call of God, he moved

out from his birthplace as the Lord had instructed him, he was not sure where God was directing him, neither was he sure what direction he was heading, but he believed that the voice he heard was that of God, and that was enough evidence for him to obey, and follow, regardless of what anyone else said. God knows who we are and where we live and whether we are near or far from him.

Abraham and his father's house would be an object of criticism and condemnation for practicing sorcery, if he was around today; because his father not only made idols he worshipped them as well. They would be ready to condemn him even though God did not. Man looketh on the outward appearance but God sees the heart.

People's judgement and condemnation of Terah would be based on the commandment that says, "Thou shalt have no other God beside me". The Ten Commandments was given to prevent Abraham and his seed from making idols now that they all knew Yahweh is real.

God saw in Abraham the ingredients of a perfect patriarch, although he was the son of an idol maker and worshipper, yet he covenanted with him because he was flexible and had the right attitude.

The fulfilment of the covenant God made with Abraham was to have started in Isaac who was not yet born, but the irony of that is that although the promise should start then, but he could have slain the lad if God was not watching Abraham's every step. People under God's covenant are also under the constant watchful eyes of God. Abraham believed that God would raise the lad from the dead even if he had killed him when he reached for the knife. Abraham's attitude and behaviour and respect for God have always been impeccable, but this time he excelled himself. He reverenced God with the ultimate respect and reverence God is worthy of, or anyone could ever show to the ultimate object of worship. He wanted to present Yahweh to the world as the true and living God that he is, not like those his father worshipped in Ur.

Isaac, like his father Abraham was fully committed to the worship of Yahweh. He wanted to show the same obedience, respect and reverence to God as his father did.

The faith which Christians' employ in worshipping God and praising Jesus, is coming from the same vein as that which Abraham and his offspring draws theirs from, that faith makes it easy to worship and praise God just as if he was physically here. Abraham's faith brought God at close range and his obedience to him endorsed that.

Obedience to God's word is therefore essential, because it is the key to the storehouse of God's blessings which includes everlasting life, anything short of this is worthy of condemnation, it is mistrust. God must be fully trusted otherwise you are calling

Him a liar, and when you trust him with your whole heart and soul and mind you cannot doubt him. When you trust God you obey him and the only way you can prove your love for God is to do what he says.

Abraham's obedience to God's word proves the everlasting promise of blessings, that was promised to Abraham and his seed, if they believe and trust him. God was not looking for a person who was rich, powerful and famous, nor was he looking for a superstar; if that was the case he would not have chosen Abraham because he was none of these. He was looking for and found in Abraham a man with charisma and obedience, to be the leader of God's righteous nation.

The name of Abraham is historically known throughout the Christian world, as the father of the Jewish nation, because of the respect he had for Yahweh and the trust he had in him from the start. As a result of that he was exhaled by God and became worthy of the highest accolade given by God, to faithful and obedient men. Abraham's obedience to God exceeds any sacrifice he has ever made, including his attempt to offer his son Isaac on Mount Moriah, all this was because he realised that to obey God is better than any other sacrifice human will ever make.

The bible says that willingness and obedience are the two most important recipes for a long life. Apart

CHRISTIAN DEVELOPMENT AND MATURATION

from obedience, willingness was one of the virtues that made Jesus sacrifice his life on Calvary where he suffered atrocious cruelty for man's redemption, for which he said just before he was crucified *"never the less not my will but thine"*.

The act of obedience cannot easily be described by ordinary words of human tongue; neither can it be explained by the most learned, using their most profound gift of expression. The mystery of God is passed finding out by human greatness, when he told Abraham that he was going to make him great; the word great in this context meant the great incentive that is imbedded in the promise that motivated Abraham's decision to get up and go. This was no ordinary act of faith, such faith is the gift of God given to anyone who will pay the price and dare to obey God the way Abraham did.

On the other hand, Jesus knew what was going to happen to him from the start; he knew the extent of the agony he would have to bear. He saw his flesh being torn from his own body down to the bare bones by the metal thongs, the Romans used to administer punishment. He saw his blood running like water down Golgotha's hill, yet he was willing to go all the way through this not for his friends or relations but for his enemies.

Is there anyone who is prepared to undergo the suffering Jesus suffered for a friend or the dearest on earth to them? I hardly think so, yet he suffered most severely for you and I, we should therefore be prepared to suffer in the same way as he suffered for us willingly, that is boundless love. Obedience of this kind starts at Calvary and ends when you die, and we know what the reward at the end is going to be.

The disciples were severely punished and threatened with further punishments if they continued preaching the gospel in the name of Jesus, the bible declares that they were ready not only to be punished but also ready to die for what they believed, rather than obeying man's threatening words and live. We must also remember that these threats were coming from ordinary men who were motivated by Satan to try and hinder the work of God.

We have many graphic pictures on record of the same extreme courage, determination and boldness of ordinary men and women like you and I who had rather suffered and died obeying God, rather than to live a few extra days on earth and loose their souls in hell, because of the lack of commitment to what they believe.

Abraham and other spiritual champions are dead but their heroic pictures are now hanging in the hall of fame in the kingdom of God as evidence of their faith and trust in God, they are now awaiting our arrival, but before we can get there and be decorated like them; we must prepare ourselves to suffer in the same way they did.

Chapter 3

FAITH AND PRAYER

Faith is the substance of things hoped for and the evidence of things not seen. This is one of the most graphic descriptions of faith written in the bible. Faith is an abstract and so is prayer, both works together forming the main channel through which man can reach God. Faith and prayer are therefore the mediums through which people of all nations on earth in their respective community have always communicated with God.

In prayer we utter words in faith and assert God of our need for his divine help, in doing so effectually and fervently, we find the solutions for all our problems as the bible says;

"The effectual fervent prayer of a righteous man availed much," (James 5:16 KJV) therefore a person who prays such prayer gets the answers to them and realises that the saying is true; but the one on its own is futile, both goes together. For what good is it my brothers, if a man claims to have faith but has no deeds, can such a faith help him? (see James 2:17 TLB)

The spiritual relationship between God and man is based on faith like that of an earthly father and his children. Children know their parent very well from experience and by the things they do for them. They know that even if they are not being good, they will get what they need and asked for, from them without prompting. If ordinary mortals can show to their children such care and understanding, God is far more loving and caring than the kindest of all earthly fathers.

God's children should ask him in confidence for what they need and especially for what he promised according to his divine will, he is obliged to fulfil his promise because he is bound by his word, the only thing that is above him.

Christians know that their heavenly Father will do as he always does, answer their prayers in one of three ways; yes, no or wait, but the only problem here is to know which of them his answer is, because anxiety plays havoc with people who are desperate. Otherwise only doubt can stand in the way of God answering sincere prayers. God has a way to surprise us at times; he answers our prayers even when we pray doubting.

The story is told of a Christian woman who was a very good seamstress but with little faith. Her sewing machine was her only source of living because she

CHRISTIAN DEVELOPMENT AND MATURATION

used it to make clothes for people. Her machine became worn out and could hardly cope with the bulk of work she had coming in; she could not afford to buy a new one so she asked God for a second hand one to replace the old one. To her amazement and surprise her prayer was answered and she got a new machine, she exclaimed, "my God if I knew I was going to get it I would have asked for a new one instead of a second hand one." This should be a lesson to everyone who prays to God asking for his favour, but at the same time doubting. Faith is what you believe, God is concerned with how you can use your faith, the more faith you have the more you can get from God's storehouse.

Patience is another important virtue; it forms a trio with faith and works. The apostle Paul declares "*but we glory in tribulation also; knowing that tribulation worketh patience; and patience experience, and experience, hope.*" (*Romans 5:3-4 KJV*).

To know Jesus Christ as ones personal saviour is an experience that is peculiar and unique to the person who is having it, this experience includes several trials and sufferings at times that only God can help you out of. Trials and testing are important and essential for spiritual growth. Some growth comes slowly but they carry integrated experiences, which only the believer will have at the end of the period of testing. Testing on the other hand are intermittent incidents along the path to priceless experience. You need these experiences when you get to the place where you have to put out the fiery darts the devil throws at you, and these often comes when you seem to be at your weakest point; it is then you realise that you are wearing the whole armour of God which the hymn writer encourages us to wear night and day.

The young Christian of today lacks all of these experiences at the start of their journey to maturation, and will accumulate them as they grow in stature and acquire them gradually. Spiritual maturation does not happen over night, it comes slowly over many years. There are many bible characters whose record and testimony of their courage and determination we now are able to draw from and encourage ourselves with their strength and bravery long after they have died and gone. We too should endeavour to leave something on record for our successors to glean from after we are gone. If we fail to do so they will be impoverished of the experience we have gleaned from the faith of our fathers. If we did not have their experiences to draw on, it would be difficult for us to get as far as we have, so we should leave our footprints on the sands of time for our successors to follow.

The apostle Paul had many years of unpleasant experiences, which involved cruelty of the most severe kind yet he was so proud to suffer for Jesus that he wrote about them as if it was a pleasure for him. He was flogged over forty six times, he was imprisoned many times, he was involved in a terrible shipwreck which almost took his life and many other incidents of which he wrote proudly *"I have fought a good fought, I have finished my course and have kept the faith. Henceforth is laid up for me a crown of righteousness which the Lord the righteous judge shall give me at that day; and not to me only, but unto all them also that love his appearing."* (2 Timothy 4:7-8).

When we consider Jesus' attitude towards prayer, we observed that though he himself was both Lord and God, because he was in the Father and the Father was in him, (*John 14:10-11*) yet he spent a lot of time praying to the Father, and we notice from those events he always went into prayer on his own. We have not seen him having prayers with his disciples even if he took a few of them along with him on his way to pray; he withdrew himself from where they were and went away to pray on his own. This suggest to me that prayer on most cases is a personal thing and it is done best when it is done on a personal level. Amazingly inasmuch as his disciples were always present in almost all the miracles that Jesus did and they were never present with him in his devotion times, yet they asked him to teach them to pray instead of doing miracles.

My opinion is that whenever Jesus returned from his devotional times in prayer with the father, they must have noticed something special about him; and they wanted to know the secret of that anointing. Then when Jesus answered their request he pointed them to observe the Fatherhood of God and that they should approach him as children, with due respect and adoration. *Matt 6:9-11* pointed out to them that in like manner as children asked their parents for the things they desire, they should adopt the same attitude of childlikeness in forgiving one another in the same way, as they needed to forgive, *verse 12-13.*

Procedure in Prayer

1. Adoration An act of paying honour to a divine being, showing regard with reverent devotion and affection. *Rom 8:28.* This act of worship is done to show our love and respect for the one who has given his life to save us from our sins; life has meaning and purpose and therefore demands our adoration and worship.

2. Confession To make confession of one's faults *1 John 1:9.* Confession does not depend on ones mood or feelings, the time to confess is immediately upon realising that we have sinned and it should be done in reality and honestly, in accepting God's forgiveness, they should also change their behaviour accordingly, if God has forgiven our sins and cleanses our unrighteousness then there must be a change in our attitude; great men of the bible as Moses and David, they were not perfect men but they were men with the ability to confess and be restored back to fellowship and went on to walk with God. We too can learn lessons from them and go on walking with God.

3. Thanksgiving is an act of giving thanks to God expressing gratitude to him not only in good times but also in times of adversities. *Eph 5:20.*

4. Supplication is Praying to God in humble petition and entreaty – supplication is in two forms, intersession for others and petitions which is for all who are in need, *Rom 15:30-32.* Paul left us an example as to how we should pray for one another, Christian believers would do well if early in their Christian life they encourage an attitude of setting up prayer partnership with other Christians where they can have other Christian groups praying for them, as well as they have you praying for them, this could bring you closer together and make you more co-operative and more successful as a church. Every Christian should have other Christians praying for them on a regular basis. It is amazing that the Almighty God allowed ordinary human beings like you and I to have intimacy with him through our prayers, and if He allowed this, then we in turn should do all in our power to maintain working relationship with our brothers and sisters in the body of Christ (the Church) in praying for each other on a regular basis.

FAITH AND PRAYER

Promise to Prayer: There are seven promises to prayer that I would like to share with you.

1. Jer 33:3 Call upon me and I will answer thee and show thee great and mighty things which thou knowest not.

2. Matt 21:22 And all things whatsoever ye shall ask in prayer believing ye shall receive.

3. 1 John 5:14-15 This is the confidence we have in him, that if we ask anything according to his will he heareth it, and if we know that he heareth us, whatsoever we ask we know that we will have the petition that we desire of him.

4. Phil 4:19 My God shall supply all your needs according to his riches in glory by Christ Jesus.

5. Psalm 84:11 The Lord God is a sun and shield, the Lord will give thee grace and glory no good thing will he withhold from them that walk uprightly.

6. Prov 3:6 In all thy ways acknowledge him and He shall direct thy ways.

7. Isa 41:10 Fear not for I am with thee, be not dismayed for I am thy God, I will strengthen thee yea I will help thee, yea I will uphold thee with the right hand of my righteousness.

These seven promises to prayer closed with a statement in question. *Rom 8:32* He that spareth not his own son but delivered him up for us all, how shall he not with him freely give us all things?

It is not the will of our loving heavenly father that those who believed in him and trusted him should live in poverty, when he sendeth rain and watered the ground of the unjust and the wicked people while sending rain on the land of those who are good. We should not doubt God, He always keeps his promises what He says He will do trust Him, He will do it, hold Him at his word.

He is a God that cannot lie, however it is important for us to observe that promises are always conditional. Note *Matt 21:22 "and all things whatsoever ye shall ask in prayer believing ye shall receive"*.

This is why it is also important that Christians should consider themselves children of God and as such, they should have childlike attitudes of faith. When you make a promise to a child, they do not question your honesty, or your ability to keep and fulfil the offer that you made. They have every confidence that you will make good your promises and are prepared to wait, as long as it takes for you to make good your promises, they never forget. So don't be surprised if they approach you several times in one day asking you if you haven't got it or if you remembered that you promised to give them something. But as long as you haven't told them that the promise is off or you will not be able to fulfil it they will always be holding you at your word.

That is the attitude of a childlike faith in prayer, and if you are praying with the intention to move the

FAITH AND PRAYER

hand of God in answering your prayer you need to pray in childlike faith every time that you prayed.

Chapter 4

─────────

LOVE FOR GOD AND OUR

FELLOWMEN

Love and discipleship are inseparable. The disciples were first called Christians in a place called Antioch; this was because of the genuine love they showed each other, not what they said.

Love is therefore not what you say it's what you do. To show his love for mankind, God sent his only Son to die and the only obligation we have is to believe on Jesus as the Saviour. *For God so loved the world that he gave his only begotten son, that whosoever believes on him should not perish but have everlasting life; John3: 16.*

The hallmarks of love are manifested in the deeds of love. The deeds of love are the same as the fruits of the spirit, which the bible says, are love, joy, peace, long suffering, gentleness, goodness, faith, meekness and self-control. It also says that love is kind and suffers long, and is not boastful, proud or selfish, *Gal 5:22-23.*

From the list above it is absolutely clear that a person's neighbour is not the person who lives next door to you or the one with whom one has a strong friendship with, ones neighbour is the person whom you show human kindness beyond ordinary human capability to express without expecting something in return. It is a God-given gift to serve each other and express itself in inexplicable human kindness regardless of colour, race or religion.

The Good Samaritan was called good, not just because he rescued the man that was on the Jericho Road, he was called good because he showed kindness that the Priest and the Levite should have shown but never did. He took him on his donkey and brought him to an inn, fed him, and bathed his wounds and offered to pay all other expenses before he continued on his journey. That was unconditional love only a person like the Good Samaritan has had.

Another graphic example of true Christian love was demonstrated in the first recorded Christian martyr who was Stephen. Under the impact of the stones of hatred and misunderstanding hurled at him by his own kinsman, instead of asking for God's judgement upon his assailants he asked for God's mercy; *"Lord do not charge them with this sin" Acts 7:60.* Only a Christian with the love of God in their heart could utter those words under the impact of the stones of hatred. This is a typical portrayal of love in action. Loving God therefore must demonstrate itself unwavering love for ones fellow men no matter who they are.

Love is one of the main virtues that all Christians must have and truly practice. Loving God with all one's heart, soul, mind and one's fellow men as ones self are the ingredients of the new commandment that Jesus prescribes for the true Christian life. The Apostle Paul in his summary about the values of love says that there are three dimensions comprising the virtue of love, faith, hope and love but the greatest of these three is love. Therefore having love, which is a divine virtue, we are fully equipped and qualified for the righteousness, which is contained in the Laws of Moses, but we need to show it. Now that love is everlasting, we look forward to the ultimate reward awaiting us who get to heaven.

Christians must show their love for each other by the way they treat one another and the unity that binds them together, evidence of that binding love must be there for all to see in the sanctuary as well as in public; if it is there it should come from the heart and manifest itself in the open. Love is kind and forgiving, it is merciful and enduring. These are some of the characteristic of love when you are born again, you now have the capacity to hold and retain the love attributes of your Father in heaven

Love for God and Our Fellowmen

and expressed it in the way it was meant to be. The natural man cannot show genuine love and kindness to his enemy nor can he forgive those who trespass against him, it takes God's love in ones heart to do these things.

Loving God and my fellowmen is not hard if I am fully committed to the faith, but it is not easy either. Christians must be genuine and sincere, if you find it quite difficult to love your fellowmen yet at the same time say that you love God, I find that quite difficult to accept because you have never seen God; you can see me because I am real. God is not visible but He is real, if you cannot love me who is seen how can you love God who is not seen! It is true that many people are hard to love because of their attitude, but if Christians are to show what makes them different from ordinary people, they must prove it by their deeds and not just words. We must be able to love the person that does not love us, anyone can love those who love them, and the test is proven when under difficult situations; if I can treat a person nice after I am treated with contempt and if I can respond with words and deeds of kindness I am on my way to being like Christ.

The issue about Christians and their fellowmen is not just about getting people to come to church for the sake of coming to make up the numbers in the pew, the ultimate objective of all true genuine and sincere Christians is to rescue peoples soul from

CHRISTIAN DEVELOPMENT AND MATURATION

hell and God's eternal punishment.

This was the reason why Jesus came and suffered and died for all of us, he did so in order to offer people the opportunity to escape the devil's hell, and live in God's heaven forever where there is no suffering or death or war or hunger. Heaven is a place where Jesus will be the eternal Lord and the saints and angels worship him forever.

In this chapter on Love for God and our fellowmen, I want to tried and point out why we should love God superior to the way we love our fellowmen around us and I hope I had made my point clear about that. However; there is something more that I would like to share on that subject and this is borne out of *John 15*, where Jesus described himself as the true vine and his Father as the Gardener or the cultivator, and the effort made between father and son to establish a sound foundation for those branches that abides in the vine and how the branches automatically produced much fruit. The verses I am referring to from this chapter is *John 15:1 – 17.* It bears out a united contact between God the Father and Jesus Christ our Lord and Saviour and the Christian believers. *Verses 1 –7 describe* Jesus as the vine and his Father as the gardener or the cultivator and the connection between the vine and branches and telling us that this unity of purpose brings glory to God who is the Creator.

The verses *9 – 17* went on to describe what I

called united love, *verse 9 "as the father loved me so have I loved you, continue in my love." Verse 10* tells of conditions to observe in order to maintain love, *verse 11* tells us that Jesus wants his followers to have real joy in being members of his team, that is why he revealed to them the things that will secure their joy, and the number one thing to keep Christian believers joyful is loving God and their fellowmen.

This vision of unity love between Jesus and his father carried down to us his followers, revealed so clearly to ordinary human beings like you and I as seen from these verses of *John 15:1-17* showing God's love to mankind sending His Son to make himself equal with sinful human being, in order to save us from our sins and unite us together with himself; making friends of us this is truly marvellous. It is even more marvellous because we who He saved from sin, we too can be united together as friends, fellow shipping together and working together to build the kingdom of God here among us; people who had never met before, whatever their nationality, black or white working together with one purpose in mind, building the kingdom of God here on earth. Praise God; thank God for such unity love that binds us together in oneness of purpose.

This brings me to a dream I had a couple of years ago, I dreamt of passing a place where I smelt a sweet odour coming from an area where there was neither flowers nor anyone insight but the fragrance

CHRISTIAN DEVELOPMENT AND MATURATION

lasted for a very long time, then after a while on my journey I caught up with a group of people on their way going to the same place where I was going, and we began to talk. The distance to travel was very far but our conversation were friendly and interesting and as we walked along sharing thoughts together we also shared what we had to eat and drink with each other, it seemed as if we were together for some long time and had all things in common, as was mentioned in the book of Acts in the time of the early church. This time of fellowship with folks I met on this journey developed into a loving friendship and the joy I shared with that company now remind me of the verse in *John 15:11*, about joy remained in you and that your joy might be full.

This life is like an uphill struggle but the love of God and the fellowship of the saints can produce joy that nothing else can, I am not here to tell you that the Christian believers does not have some hard and difficult times, even among ourselves, but the blood of Jesus Christ still prevails and it prevails best when Christians learned to humble themselves and obey God's word; words like *John 15:4-5 "abide in me and I in you as the branch cannot bear fruit of itself, except it abide in the vine, neither can we except we abide in Christ", verse 5 " I am the vine ye are the branches, ye that abideth in me and I in him the same bringeth forth much fruit for without me ye can do nothing".*

LOVE FOR GOD AND OUR FELLOWMEN

Remember Christians have not chosen the Lord, it is God who has chosen us and appointed us to do service for Him and our fellowmen around us. It is upon our faithful services in response to the service we are called to fulfil, whatever we asked of the Father using the name of Jesus His Son, He promises to give it to us.

Christians are quick to quote the promises of God and so we should but thank God the promises of God do not have small print attached, all God's promises are written in one size print so let us not quote them to suit ourselves; let us use them as they are and if we are not sure of its true meaning there is always a Pastor or a lay person in all our churches who you can find to help you to understand the scriptures. Furthermore do make a practice of having regular devotion time with the Lord, a time when you can shut yourself in with God in reading the bible and praying prayers to him. All Christians who took this exercise find it very profitable so will you, try it and you will be glad you did.

Most of the revelations and ideas I got and used in this book comes from times of my devotions with the Lord down through the years; these are the times when we take our difficult cases to the Lord in prayer, all of our ifs and whys and uncertainties to the throne of grace and discovered God's love and compassion; these are the times when we experienced like David in his *Psalm 46* that God is a refuge and strength and a present help in times of troubles. It takes times of constant meeting with someone to build up friendship and you do that better when you meet them on their own not in the presence of other people. The same is true with the Lord, all personal relationships developed alone with some one privately, even a child knows that.

Can I tell you a little more about my vision of unity love? Unity love is like an ever growing fruit tree constantly bearing fruit all seasons of the year, blooming with flowers all the time, its flowers gives out sweet fragrance, spreading out to distance around, attracting viewers to it from far and near as the news of its aroma spreads, it attracts visitors from everywhere.

This unity love in my vision not only attracts visitors for its fragrance, but its fruits are equally sought after, people are always talking about unity love when they come into contact with it, because of its scarceness. It is in great demand and since good things are usually scarce, when they get hold of it they try to hold onto it as long as they can, in order to get the full benefit from it.

The idea of unity love can attract some wishful thinking but unity has never been achieved solely because people wish for it, for unity to become practical; effort has to be made to get it established and working. Those interested in working together on a project must have an imaginary plan as a blue print to show others the plan you have in mind, that is vision, a plan is not always prepared by a vast number of people, it could be by just one or a few people to draw out the plan and introduce it to others with the hope that it will be accepted by all.

Preparing the ground for unity of purpose can be costly but the person with the vision generally is the one to foot the bill, which can be seen from the scripture mentioned in *John 15*. Jesus declares Himself as the vine and His father the cultivator and *John 3:16* gives the foundation of unity love, God gave Jesus to prepare the ground on which the vine grew and provides branches on which unity love keeps growing all the time. We might not admit the fact that unity is thriving, because of the slowness of its growth among us as Christians, but the fact that the gospel of the Kingdom of God is spreading around the world; now more than any other time in the history of mankind. This is evidence that unity love is at work somewhere, and my advice to the people of God is that since there is evidence that there are people who are united to take the gospel around the world; to me this is enough proof that people are showing their love for God and their fellowmen who are dying in their trespasses and sin by trying to reach them with the gospel, which is the power of God unto salvation to them that believe it.

Now having seen that unity love is at work and is making success, let's do our part by making some

CHRISTIAN DEVELOPMENT AND MATURATION

meaningful contributions to keep the project going. There are various ways to support the project and my prayer is that God through the Holy Spirit will inspire our hearts to do that which pleases God.

In closing this chapter Christian Love for God and our Fellowmen, I leave you with *Eph 5:29* the purpose of nourishing someone is to make them thrive in abundant living unto everlasting life with Christ. *John 3:16* is the total sum of Unity Love for the Lord; my destination is everlasting life with Christ, what about you?

Chapter 5

CHRISTIAN WORSHIP

A woman who was of low moral and socially not acceptable was in conversation with Jesus who was on his way back to Jerusalem from a very special mission. She was a worshipper of the Hebrew God Yahweh, but was not sure who this God was. She knew the Torah very well as was indicated by her in the conversation with Jesus. The conversation was about the subject of worship, in that important meeting and the following conversation, she told Jesus that the mountain on that part of Samaria near to the place where they were talking was the place where men should worship, Jesus told her that the Jews worship Yahweh by covenant promise, but the time has come when true worshippers, regardless of race, colour or religion should worship God in spirit and in truth (*John 4:5-24*).

Christian worship is an integral part of Christianity; it begins at conversion and continues throughout the

CHRISTIAN DEVELOPMENT AND MATURATION

Christian life on earth. It starts again after the rapture and continues throughout eternity. Worshiping God is the duty of all God's creation on earth as well as in heaven; people were made to worship and worship we will. Some worship various idols with different significance but regardless of the motive behind the worship they worship. The bible says that God made all things for his glory and the whole duty of man is to worship *(Isa 43:7, Ecc 12:13)*.

The heavenly hosts render their services to God continuously because they were created exclusively for that purpose. A person who is born again consciously worships God after conversion to show their gratitude to God for his mercies during their life of ungodliness. The psalmist David was Israel's most revered king; on realising the uniqueness of the body, soul and spirit of man concluded that man was fearfully and wonderfully made. *(Psalm 139:14)* This uniqueness of man and the gratitude he chooses to render to his creator makes man a subject of praise to the object of worshipping God. Solomon was King David's favourite son, Solomon's conclusion was that the whole duty of man is to fear God and keep his commandments *(Ecc 12:13)*.

Man is therefore required to perform holy duty forever to God because like the angels, worship is the purpose for which man was made. Man made to serve and serve he will, man was given the power of choice from the day he transgressed God's law;

he has the power of choice of what and where to worship. This power of choice means that man has given himself options for his own pleasure, to worship or not to worship a question he alone must answer. The multi-choice of objects for worship gives man the right to choose, but this does not give him freedom from the responsibility to worship the Almighty God although man will continue to worship what he likes.

There are many issues regarding the worship of God which we do not understand, but what we understand from the bible is that angels and other heavenly hosts are constantly chanting the praises of God and the Lamb, because they unlike some men, realise that Jesus is worthy and they worship him as such. Man serves and worships various objects because they believe the object of worship will provide gratification and lasting satisfaction to them, but their soul and spirit will never be satisfied until the vacuum that God created inside man is occupied by God himself.

Worship is the only service that the born again believer is expected to render to Jesus, as long as the believer remains faithful to God and his word. He is promised resurrection from the grave and eternal life after that. There is nothing else that the Christian is asked to do except witnessing to the uncommitted, telling them of the unfathomable love and grace of God that brought salvation to all men.

CHRISTIAN DEVELOPMENT AND MATURATION

There are times when you feel as if you are riding on cloud nine and you have no care at all in the world. You find consolation and solace in every song that kept springing up in your heart like a refreshing spring ready to overflow its banks. There are other times when you feel as if the world is on top of you and you are about to cave in, when you find yourself in this situation you cannot find a song to cheer you or a word to comfort you from anyone. These are times when worship is not as easy as before, but these are the best times to praise and worship God, anyone can sing when the sun is shining but it takes God almighty himself to bring back to your remembrance things he has brought you through, and reminds you that he can do it again.

Christian worship is also the attitude whereby we express profound gratitude and adoration to God alone. There are other forms of worship to other objects, but true worship belongs to God and him alone. Christian worship is not ordinary it is special, it is an exclusive devotion given continuously to God by his people who have personal experience of him and who have a testimony about him and the new birth.

To such people worship is inevitable because what they are doing is showing gratitude to God for his work of grace and mercy shown to them at a time when they did not deserve it. A personal experience is the motivating factor behind all praise and worship of God in continuous songs simply because the individual wants to show continuous gratitude in a most significant way. Christian worship is significant of a person who was almost drowning in deep waters but after going down for the last time they were extremely grateful because it was at the last moment he was rescued by someone he did not know. Only the most ungrateful person would forget such kindness at such a critical moment.

Who can receive of God's mercy and grace and not rejoice at receiving it. Solomon the wisest man asked the question; can a man put out a live coal in his bosom and remain still? When one experiences the love of God in ones heart one cannot stay still except one is dead.

In heaven right now there are hosts of angels in their various ranks and in innumerable numbers, performing rapturous and glorious service to their creator doing their normal duties, but we are told that when the redeemed get there the heavenly hosts will have no option but to fold their wings in silence when they hear the redeemed singing their songs of redemption in their presence. Whether they will join in the singing we are not able to definitely say, but it will be more glorious than anything ever experienced by anyone anywhere. We are told that no one, in spite of our present technological time, will be able to count the number of the saints that will comprise the mass choir that will render their praises to God and Jesus for ever. The angels, the elders and the heavenly host will not be able to worship God as the saints will, because they were created primarily to minister to the redeemed that are the seeds of Abraham long before the advent of Jesus Christ *(Heb 2:14-18)*.

Chapter 6

CHRISTIAN WITNESS

A witness is one who has personal knowledge of an event or incident that occurred at sometime, either once or several times, one is able to give evidence of something seen or heard. A Christian witness then, is one who has personal knowledge of salvation and is able to give evidence of their coming into salvation and what salvation has done for them or to them. They should also be able to tell what is the source of their Christianity.

The title of this book is Christian Development & Maturation. Development comes in stages in order to be matured, these stages are called processes; hence the Christian believer would have passed through some process in order to be a witness. Witnessing of itself is a process of ongoing changes to the extent that Jesus advised his disciples to tarry in Jerusalem until they were filled with power from on high, before they go out to witness as seen in *Luke 24:49. Acts 1:8* tells us that when the Holy

CHRISTIAN DEVELOPMENT AND MATURATION

Ghost is come upon them they shall be witnesses unto him both at home and in Jerusalem and unto other parts of the world; Therefore it is evident from these scriptures that Christian witnesses should be people with ability to deliver evidence of what they have seen or have knowledge of.

When Peter stood up on the day of Pentecost being filled with the Holy Spirit as Jesus told them they would be, and having the boldness to defend the rest of brethren declaring that they were not drunk but what they saw happening was the fulfilment of prophecy spoken by the prophet Joel many years before. Then Peter continued to give a history of things being done and said by prophets of old, so what was happening on that day was only confirmation to what was prophesied before.

Of a truth one can always rely on the words of Jesus, whenever he made a statement of things that will happen, they generally come to pass. He told the disciples to tarry for the Holy Ghost in *Luke 24:49* as mentioned earlier, now we have seen that the disciples obeyed his word as can be seen in *Acts 2:1*, then came the outpouring of the Holy Spirit in verses *2-4* and verses *5-13* tells of the confusion among the people in the area; they were not accustomed to seeing anything like this before, they were frightened and confused. Nevertheless God's timing is always right for every occasion, the statement made in verses *5-6* declared that there were a number of people living around the area where this strange event took place, compounded with the spreading of the news of the incidents, causing a greater ingathering of people on the scene the place where it happened, making it possible for multitudes of people to be gathered at one place at the same time, making it a unique opportunity for an evangelism campaign for Peter who now being filled with the power of the Holy Spirit, seized the opportunity to preach his greatest sermon. This resulted in the harvest of a great number of souls into the kingdom of God (3,000) altogether.

Whenever there is an active move of the Holy Spirit in a Christian group of believers, evangelism is usually one of the chief product resulting, because Jesus gave the commission of evangelism to the disciples, so then it is equally given to Christians of today. I make this statement without a shadow of doubt in my mind, because the fact that Jesus expects his followers, the Christian church, the born again believers to witness to their faith in God through Jesus Christ the Lord. All who witness should have the same goal in mind and that is to make Jesus a reality to all the people around us and if so, then we all should make evangelism a priority. Our aim must be to influence others to come and share Jesus with us.

It can be argued that evangelism is a gift of the Spirit given to some members of the church, making them more qualified for the task. This could also be said of those people in *Matt 25* who were given talents to trade on. In that parable each person got a different amount of talents, but even the one with only one talent was not exempt from trading on what he got, as can be seen in that scripture *Matt 25:14-30*. And if so, then I can only accept that all of us who are called by God, converted, born again and become members of the body of Christ, are called to witness to His glory and that witness includes evangelism.

Jesus has clearly stated that those receiving the power of the Holy Spirit would be able to witness of Him, see *Acts 1:8*. We see the first evidence of that displayed in *Acts 2* as mentioned earlier, with Peter's witness and its accomplishment. We further see in other chapters of the Acts of the Apostles where the disciples continued their witnesses and many people were healed, sight was restored to the blind, the church was united together, believers learned to share what they had with each other; giving them the opportunity to have things in common; breaking down barriers between rich and poor.

We even noticed that these united conditions among the people of God did not prevent the devil from showing up among them and we can see in *Acts 5*, where he showed up when Ananias and his wife Sapphira sold land following the pattern set by other brethren, but when their land was sold their problems began. Satan turned up and prevailed in getting them to cheat, holding back a part of the money that they got from the sale of the land. Equally as Satan showed up, the Holy Spirit was present also, and revealed to Peter that the couple had cheated, giving them the chance to change their mind and to repent, but they refused to change their minds and repent, not realising how great the power of the Holy Spirit is. They fell victim of their own deceit and dropped dead before the man of God (Peter), one after the other and were taken up and buried.

This is a lesson for the believers in Christ that when the spirit of God is actively present amongst the people of God, the devil also is present among us and is ready to make a prey of anyone who is not sanctified, thus causing them to be deceitful enough to destroy themselves. Therefore believers in Christ should endeavour to guard themselves with the word of God and pray earnestly for the sanctifying power of God to keep us from falling victim to the devil. It is to this end the word of God entreats us to be strong in the Lord and in the power of his might *Eph 6:10.*

As I write this to my readers I am reminded in scriptures of the many times that we read in the book of Acts, where the disciples were filled with the Holy Ghost and at those times they did extraordinary things to the Glory of God, which suggest that their success in witnessing, was due to their own

CHRISTIAN DEVELOPMENT AND MATURATION

continual infilling of the Holy Spirit and if the Church of God in the 21st century, want similar success, we like them must earnestly contend for the faith and power that they had and this is possible because the same Jesus that they had as their source of faith and power, we in our day and time have the same access to the same Jesus as the scripture tells us in *Heb 13:8. He is the same yesterday, today and will be forever.*

There are a few of us living today who can recall of instances when we were younger, that we have seen men and women who trusted God and how God has used them in many ways and has answered their prayers in healing the sick, restoring sight to people who we knew couldn't see for some long period of time, providing food and clothing for some poor people, making life a lot more easier for them. In those days things and conditions of life were not as good as the average people have it today; but it has always been the same for the Christians and people who served God and testified of Him as their Saviour; they are always the ones who are happy even if they don't have a lot of material things or money, they are always singing and praising God.

I can remember even my own mother, the times when she gathered us around her bedside at least every Sunday morning when we were children for devotional reading of the Bible. She would share the word of God with us the way she knew it; she would council us and warned us to be good children. She taught us to have respect for older people and that good manners make good people; and that we should be loving and kind to everybody.

Coupled with that long counselling session she went on to instruct us to pray giving thanks to God for being so good by providing food to eat, clothes to wear, a roof over our heads and any conceivable thing that came to her mind she would give thanks to God for them. This was invaluable training for later years.

As I grew older I sometimes found it hard to share her devotion meaningfully, but the seed that she has sown into my heart by the word of God from the Bible continues to germinate in my soul, to the extent that I grew to understand the scripture verse in *Prov 22:6 "Train up the child in the way that he should grow and when he is old he will not depart from it"*. In as much as I knew that I was not a converted Christian until several years later, yet due to the training I got from my mother during my childhood, I learned the fundamental principles of Christianity; knowing the difference between sin and righteousness, enough to keep me from falling into some pits and trouble which I have seen several of my friends fall into in early adolescence. Thank God for a godly mother, my mother taught me the way to be a true witness to people around me from early childhood, making it less difficult when I became a converted Christian, and thank God I was able to emulate that trait when I became a father growing my own children all seven of them, thank God.

As we read in the book of Acts we observed several successes they had due to their constant infilling of the Holy Spirit. We read in the gospel of *John 15* where Jesus talking to his followers, He told them in *verse 5 "I am the vine, ye are the branches, He that abideth in me and I in him, the same bringeth forth much fruit; for without me ye can do nothing".* In as much as Jesus was not in the flesh with his disciples during the time of the early church, He had promised to send the Holy Spirit as a comforter and as a sustainer to them when he was gone from them. The Holy Spirit was then his representative, the Holy Spirit did not take over from him, He was working alongside him completing the trinity, Father, Son and Holy Spirit. The followers of Christ knew that then and we as followers of Christ need to know it now, that without the triune God we cannot do the things that brings glory to God, and if so it is not enough to have God's help on some occasions but we need to be filled with Him because we need him all the time if we are to be successful.

While writing this article I am conscious of the fact that if this book is to be of any benefit to those reading it, it must be inspired by the Holy Spirit who will use it to inspire the heart of the reader, or else it will find its way on the shelves of people's homes only to gather dust, but with the Holy Spirit leading, everywhere, it finds itself even if the devil tried to make it counter productive, God's power will prevail and lead the reader to aspire for the good that is appropriate to their need. This is why when we are led in our spirit to do witness for the Lord, there is a constraining urge in our heart to seek God's guidance. The Psalmist tells us in *Psalm 32:8 "I will instruct thee and teach thee in the way which thou shall go, I will guide thee with my eye".* These are the driving force that leads so many of God's little people to move out of their small corners and get into the lime light and be counted.

It is not easy for people like myself to pluck courage to write their ideas to be published, there are so much discouraging factors holding you back, like myself it took me more than 45 years to pluck up the courage to write this book. I have given up on it several times but the more I went to God in prayer concerning it, is the more urge I got to do it, until, since the last couple of years it came forcible to me that my time is running out and I have not accomplished the purpose of my calling. I went to God another time in prayer and I got a vision of someone to contact, I contacted the person and told him my plan and without any hesitation he offered his assistance; hence we started the project but not without opposition, as Satan decided to thwart the plan with various setbacks. However these are all proven to be God's ways of allowing more time to get a better job done. Since the beginning of 2006 I discovered the need of re-writing one chapter and made improvements and additions to others, in this way what was intended to be sabotage became an opportunity for improvement. Thank God one more time for His guiding hand in what is being done to his praise and glory.

More and more I am convinced that the Lord is leading me to share my vision with people who will read my story, that they may be encouraged that if they have a desire to do something which can be interpreted to be to the benefit of others, first step to take is to pray about it, present it to the Lord in prayer and wait on Him for direction, do not be over anxious, if your vision is God's purpose for your life He will continue to give confirmation that will help you to make up your mind to make the right commitment at the right time.

As I write this, my mind is drawn to two sets of people, I believed that like myself, I delay so long to start writing this book, though I was convinced that God had called me to make a contribution in writing but I kept telling myself that I didn't have the ability intellectually, to do a good job of it; to the extent that I tried to dismiss it from my mind and as the years went by, I sometimes believed that I am getting a way out of having to do it. At other times I felt that I am too old to concentrate on writing, at one time I felt my nerves was going, my hands began to shake, I had to tell myself this is it, I will not be able to write enough to write a letter again, much more a book.

Since the year 2000 the urge for writing started to surface again, I went to Jamaica to visit some of my relatives; I stayed with my younger sister Gladys Russell. While I was there I came across a book that attracted my attention and started to read it. It was some 400 pages and I read it through in less than two weeks, whenever I had any spare time I couldn't avoid reading it; when I asked Gladys where she got it because I would like to get one to buy, she told me that it was I who gave it to her many years before. By the time I finished reading it I regained my urge for writing and started to make notes for this book, in addition I discovered a briefcase of notes I left with her when we were moving back to England. Some years before, I went through those notes and found enough materials to write a book. I thought then I wouldn't need to do much writing, all I would need is to get those notes typed, but when I start putting them together I found that I needed to do a lot more writing to add to those notes and as I started writing my hands were not shaking as they were earlier. I came to realise that the time when I began to make these extra notes I did pray to the Lord asking Him to steady my hands in order that I may manage to get on with my writing and the more I write was the better my writing became. This assures me that if God has called you into service, He will hold your hand and He will keep you fit to do the things needed to his Praise and Glory.

My advice to anyone who feels the call of God on your heart to do something, pray about it and continue praying until you get enough confirmation to assure you that it is God who called you to make a contribution to his service.

Secondly there are several thousands of people out in the world, living in every country, many of you have grown up in Christian homes and attended Sunday schools, some have even made commitment to the Christian faith, but as you grew older, peer pressure and other situations has robed you of your commitment; but at times you still feel a sense of hunger and thirsting for God's love to attend your life, you scarcely attended church services, but occasionally you see a religious service on the TV or you heard one on the radio. But on some occasions something interrupted and you lost your focus, maybe you have not read the Bible lately or you have not read it long enough to get it to make an impression on you, for the Holy Spirit to draw you back to the Lord, if so, here is a chance if you are reading this book you will find that the writer shared some of the conditions you experienced, but God in his great mercy and compassion has drawn me back to his fold and he can do the same for you.

I am now 86 years of age and this is the time

he is using me to write this book, so that you and others can see that God has never given up on anyone, nor do you have to go to a church meeting in order to be rescued from your sin. This writer was saved from sin through Jesus grace 50 years ago; wanting to attend a watch night service but because of the flu, I was not able to go to the meeting but at home without the influence of any Christian witness or sermon preached to me, I felt a desire for Christ in my life. I knelt down at my bedside sometime about one o'clock that new years morning and it was there my breakthrough came. In the book of *Hebrews chapter 13:8* it tells us that Jesus is the same yesterday, today and forever, I found it so then and you can find it so now, wherever you are, if you will kneel just where you are and invite Jesus Christ into your heart, what He has done for me and many others, He will do for you, because He loves you with an everlasting love whoever you are and wherever you are.

As I write, the prayer on my heart is that all who read this book with an open mind, the Spirit of God will graciously avail himself to inspire them with the appropriate blessings of their need. There is no greater blessing to anyone than that they themselves being a blessing to others.

It doesn't matter how far you have strayed from the Lord, if you are a backslider or if you had never made a decision or a commitment to follow the

CHRISTIAN DEVELOPMENT AND MATURATION

Lord, but since you are alive, it could be that God has cause you to be alive until this day, because He wants to convert you, making you a special person and to bless you that you will be a blessing to others. It doesn't matter if the life you are now living may not be a pleasant one in the eyes of other people, or even in your own eyes. God is a merciful compassionate God who loves you just as you are, and He wants to make you as good as any good person, if you know one, and if you don't know anyone who you would consider to be good, He can make you one if you will just invite him into your life to be your Saviour.

Please do it today and if you do, you will be able to join others to tell your story of what the Lord has done in your life, not only that, but you could be one of us who the Lord will use to His praise and glory.

Then you can go and share your story with people in your community.

Sharing your story can sometimes be challenging, however, in the gospel of *Mark 5* an extraordinary story is told of a man who was possessed by demons. It is amazing to know how much good can come out of what is known to be evil. In the case of this demon possessed, his condition was grievous as you can imagine with a human being under the control of evil spirits. He was using stones to do damage to himself, bruising and cutting his body, running wild and tearing off his clothes and whenever anyone got near to him trying to help him to get control of himself or to prevent him from doing himself any further damage by binding him with chains, the demons within him would break the chains or any other means used to restrain him.

But praise God, the Son of God Jesus the Almighty arrived on the scene. Then even the demons that possessed the man acknowledged the power of Jesus and begged him rather than sending them out of the country, to send them into a herd of pigs that were feeding nearby. Jesus met their request by allowing them to go into the pigs, but what they did not know was that the Son of God is not obliged to satisfy the request of demons. So in as much as he allowed them to go where they thought that they would be safe, the herd of pigs being possessed by the demons ran violently into the sea where they perished through drowning. Thankfully the man was delivered free from the grievous state that he had been in, and when he regained consciousness he was given clothes and food and became as good a person as anyone else, in the area where he lived.

When the men who took care of the pigs saw what had happened to the demon possessed man, how the demons left him and went into the pigs and they ran down the slope into the sea and were destroyed, they went into the villages around and told the villagers what they saw, and a great number of people went out to see it for themselves.

Whilst this was being done, someone went and asked Jesus to leave the scene before the owners of the pigs got there, because they will be very angry of their loss. They may want to attack Jesus for giving the demons consent to go into the herd of pigs.

Jesus on leaving the scene boarded a ship to sail away, but while he was entering on board, the man out of whom the demons had left, made a plea to Jesus to let him go along with him. Jesus objected to his request and advised him to return to his own village from which he came and tell his story of the things that befallen him, and how Jesus rescued him from his torture, and he was now returning home to tell the wonderful deliverance that he had experienced.

The man heeded the advice Jesus gave him and returned home spreading the good news as he went. The scripture *Mark 5:20* tells us that he departed and began to publish his story as he went.

The area of his mission was about 10 cities which was a federal state. In obedience he willingly went on his journey covering that vast area, telling his story with his mouth as well as living as a model which modern day Christians should emulate. That which was said of him can also be said of all of us, that all men (and I believe women too) marvelled when meeting him and hearing his story.

Our situation in sharing our story does not have to be the same as the man in *Mark 5*. He was sent on a lone mission because his circumstances were different; he was alone at the time. In most cases we work together as a group, on the mission field, or in a church, which makes the sharing of our stories even easier. But in whatever situation we are, the sharing of our story will depend on one or more of a number or things: -

a. What motivates us to tell our story,

b. How well we tell our story,

c. To whom we tell our story or how often we tell our story,

What motivates us to tell our story?

1. A story told with a passionate desire to please the person who ordered you to go and tell your story, respect for the authority of the sender and your understanding of the importance of telling your story to others, who could well be waiting to hear such a quality story. How they may marvel because they have not previously heard that kind of thing happening in their country, state, town or community. So they don't know or believe that things like your story are happening in the Christian community in

modern times. Hearing and seeing it happening next door to them can make them marvel.

2. Some of the people in our neighbourhood do believe that God is still a mighty God and powerful enough to do miracles as they read in their Bibles he did it in the past. Maybe the church where they attend now that kind of thing does not happen and they are neither hearing nor seeing them happening around them. When you arrive, telling and showing them that it is happening in your group, church or community, they may be astonished and glad to the point of wanting to join forces with you to make it happen more widely.

3. Most of us would like to see miracles happening in our church, such as divine healing every time we prayed. Then we could share our stories of divine healing, but divine healing is not the only thing going on, within our church groups or fellowships. God is always using people who are willing and obedient to bring miracles into other peoples lives, but those most likely to be used are sanctified people. People who are humble, willing and obedient, who when the Lord lays a thought in their hearts of something which needs to be done, will pray for confirmation and having received it, will go ahead and do it. God acknowledges their obedience and rewards them with a miracle.

4. Sometimes when a miracle is wrought, it is the receiver of the miracle that has to tell those that

God used, that a miracle has been done to them. For this reason it is necessary that the receiver of the miracle is also humble enough to share their experience of the things that God has done in their lives, through those who God used to be the extension of his hand reaching out to them. Quite often miracles are being done in people's lives but they keep it to themselves, too proud and selfish to share it with their brethren. They may say they tell it to the Lord and thank him for it but they are too conceited to tell it to the church that helped them to move the hand of God in performing their miracle.

5. Sometimes people testify of God's goodness to them in providing them with things, but are not humble enough to tell their story of whom the Lord used to bring about their miracle. The people of God need to be more open to one another, in order that God can use each one of them to be his hand extended in the body of Christ to which we are a part. Isaiah 1:19 tells us that if we are willing and obedient we shall eat the good of the land. This means that any good thing which belongs to the Kingdom of God, his children will have access to it, as long as they are willing, obedient, humble and thankful.

In my interest of sharing my story I have discovered a few important things that I could share with others:

i. My reason for loving God above all others. I

love God on the understanding that he loves me unconditionally. He loves me as I am not because of what I do or say about him. Even more he loves me for what he can do for me and not what I can do for myself, and all he asks of me in return, is to be humble. See again Isaiah 1:19

ii.   In contrast to the point made above people in my own and perhaps others lives, when they express their love for me or each other, it may generally be as a result of something they believe can be done for them or because something is said of them, that they wanted to hear. But if we fail, we are quickly written off or disliked. But as we share our stories there are certain things we may need to learn.

iii.   It is important to treat each other as equals, remembering that we are all subject to failure; hence we should try to be supporters of one another.

iv.   As supporters of each other we must try to encourage humility in the body of Christ. One of the reasons why we cannot tolerate each others mistakes and failures and try to help them, is that we may hold a higher estimation of ourselves and of those around us, more than those with whom we do not get along very well with. My own experience of getting along with people during my lifetime or at least since I understand how to relate to people, is that people who do not put a lot of self worth on themselves, got along with a greater number of people, regardless of social intellectual or economic status.

Having realised this I have learnt to accept people for who they are and I am developing an attitude of helping people who need me even more than I need them, not that they may grow to be dependant on me but that I can share my story with them. Sometime in my life I found it difficult to make two ends meet, even more than their situation at the moment. And that it was God who sent someone in my life to help me out of my plight, making it now possible for me to help them. And in like manner, in due time God will help them also to help others in their times of need, as we generally reap what we sow.

There is a growing need for unity in the body of Christ (the Church). The church will thrive best when there is a fellowship of goodwill amongst the believers. It happened in the early church at the very beginning of its existence, *Acts 2:41-47* and *Acts 4:31-37* as well as many other scriptures will support this. The chief source behind our unity is humbleness of spirit, soul and mind of each believer a pattern set for us by Jesus himself. As we read in *Phil 2: 4-9* and it is to this end Jesus prayed to his Father in *John 17:17* to sanctify his followers through the truth. It truly takes the humbling of spirit, soul and mind through sanctification, for us as believers in Christ to live and maintain our life stories effectively to keep people marvelled by the power of God in our lives. This is something that most of us within the body of Christ want to see and achieve, but only a few of us are willing to pay the cost.

In the story of the demonic man who Jesus healed and told him to go home and tell his story of what was done for him, which he did and those to whom he told it were amazed. This brings me to an instance in my experience some three years ago when returning from a visit to Jamaica when we arrived back home, I found an appointment letter advising me to go to the hospital to arrange for surgery to remove cataract from my eyes. I took the letter to the hospital and told the doctor that I was not prepared to go through with the surgery, he said Mr Johnson if you are not comfortable with this appointment you are free to cancel it, but it is a simple operation and you should not be afraid to go through with it, and failing to do so, it will only get worse and I should think about it. I told him I have given the matter a lot of thought and I really do not want to have it done, so I left the hospital without making any further arrangement, that was over three years ago.

The next morning while I was washing my face, the Spirit told me that I should wash my eyes and while doing so, I should say in the name of the Father, in the name of the Son and in the name of the Holy Spirit and that I should do this each time that I washed my face. Since then I make it a practice to do so as often as I remember to do it.

CHRISTIAN WITNESS

On Saturday morning the 24th June 2006, while I a was carrying out this exercise, the devil confronted me with these words, "you are only wasting your time, this will never work", I said to him, who must know better weather it will work or not, you or me? It is over 3 years since I am carrying out this exercise and my eyes hasn't got any worse. I can read almost anything and I can write almost anything without using my reading glasses at the age of 86. Satan you are a liar and will always be, this trick won't work, try another.

This story may not amaze many people, as it was in the case of the instance in Mark 5:20 but to me it is amazing how subtle the devil is, but praise God for the Holy Spirit who is always at hand to give us a ready answer sufficient for the occasion, confirming the word of Matt. 28:20 the last clause "Lo I am with you always, even unto the end of the world", Amen. Praise God for this assurance it holds good for those who believe it.

Chapter 7

SPIRIT FILLED BELIEVER

A spirit filled believer is one who experienced conversion from sin, being born again, see *John 3:3-6* and *John 4:14* which declares, the indwelling spirit as the work of grace deposited in the believer, has the potential to thrive into everlasting existence. This is made possible because they are sealed with the Holy Spirit of promise, *Ephesians 1:13*.

The Holy Spirit first convicts the heart of sin and cause it to become penitent in order that it may repent and seek forgiveness, *Psalm 51:1-2* and *Psalm 139:23-24*. He also continues to be the source of knowledge, directing the believer how to stay on track in difficult times and to keep on course when the sailing gets rough, *John 14:26* reminds us of the comforter who encourage us on our way, *John 14:16-18*.

The indwelling spirit in the believer also gives power to live godly lives as well as to do service to

God and their fellowmen, *Acts 1:8* and *Luke 24:49*. This power will enable the believer to resist the devil in times of temptation and will give boldness and courage to witness and to live holy. It is important that all born again believer accept the fact that the Holy Spirit is promised to all who believed in God, and not just only for a few people, *Joel 2:28* and *Act 2:3*.

The Holy Spirit can also be sought, *Luke 11:13*. Since the Holy Spirit is promised to all believers and that the Lord will give him to all who seek him, according to *Luke 11:13,* and there are vast benefits to be gained in having him in our lives, it is regrettable that so many people are contented to live their lives without God and the Holy Spirit. My question is, could it be that the spirit filled believers of our times are not producing enough evidence of the power of God that in fills our lives, or is it the unbelievers are waiting until they are sick or fall into trouble, for them to come and ask for prayer to heal their sickness or to get them out of their troubles?

It is so sad to think of so many of our own relatives and people, whom we get along with so nicely, are refusing to accept Jesus in their lives, but rather rely on their relatives and friends to pray to get them out of their sickness or troubles when they come along.

Troubles and sicknesses are not the only dilemmas which can befall people, the word of God declares

CHRISTIAN DEVELOPMENT AND MATURATION

in *Ecclesiastes 12:13-14 "Let us hear the conclusion of the whole matter, God must be honoured and his commandments kept, for this is the whole duty of man, for God shall bring every work into judgement, with every secret thing, whether it be good or evil".* My advice to people reading these words, is don't wait for sickness or trouble to lead you to prayer, you will not be living on planet earth forever, your life span in this life, will come to an end one day, you will have to give an account to God as to how you spend the life you had, that you did not give yourselves.

In case you say, you don't believe in God, it makes no difference whether you believe there is a God or if you don't believe, God is a reality, you will face that fact sooner or later and if you read this paragraph in this book and have not repented of your negligence by accepting God's sacrifice for your sin, when you die you will go to a place called hell, where there will be no time to change your mind then, so I plead with you, take my advice, spend a little time and think it over, if what I said here is not for you, dismiss it, but suppose it involves you? Where will you spend your long eternity?

My prayer is that you will seek the Lord while He is near and call on Him for his saving grace while He can be found. God is good and it is not his will that anyone should be lost. If you seek him you will find him and you will be glad you did, but sorry if you didn't, the choice is yours and yours alone.

Continuing on the spirit filled believers. The spirit filled believers are like a natural family with a name peculiar to that family, this peculiarity comprises of the genes, the blood and the family name, in a similar pattern, the family of God bears His name and is bonded with the blood of Jesus by which it is purified.

The family of God is a universal institution so enormous that it's members cannot be counted, see *Revelation 7:9-10*, it comprises people of every tribe and nations on the earth, all blood washed believers belong to it, and that is the reason why we are called brothers and sisters by each other.

Our heavenly Father comprises of all the virtues which made Him the greatest Father there is. The virtue of love, kindness, peace, gentleness, meekness and whatever other virtues there, and spirit filled believers should possess these virtues as part of the family of God because it is the evidence of love and unity in the family that attract people to God and of course unity brings oneness and co-operation and where there is unity there is strength.

This is where the Christian family is different from the non-Christian family, in spite of it's family name and genes there are sometimes great rifts, which divides the family, whereas the family of God may have differences of opinion from time to time but the

CHRISTIAN DEVELOPMENT AND MATURATION

rule of the family is not to let the sun go down before those differences are settled.

To the natural man these things are impossible, but to the spirit filled believers it is not easy but necessary and possible because the indwelling spirit deposited in us has the potential to keep us from falling victim to the pressure of the devil, for *"we are more than conquers through him that loved us"* Romans 8:37.

The spirit filled believer has no fear of evil or the power of Satan, because the evil that exist is subject to the spirit that is in the believer, and the word of God tells us that *"greater is He that is within us than he that is in the world"* 1 John 4:4 and Isaiah 54:17 tells us *"that no weapon formed against us shall prosper"*.

The spirit filled believers are known to be successful even to the laying down of their lives in death, as in the case of Stephen in *Acts 7:57-60*. From the time of Pentecost when the spirit fell upon the believers and they were all filled with the Holy Spirit, and Peter had an extraordinary anointing to preach the gospel where about 3,000 souls were saved, until this present time is the dispensation of the Holy Spirit who is confirming and performing the work and miracles of God with signs following the work, and service of the believers to the glory of our heavenly Father.

The family of God does not only share the infilling of the Holy Spirit in their lives, but there are other blessings that are available to us, blessings such as gifts of the spirit as mentioned in *Romans 12* and also *1 Corinthians 12*, but many believers are ignorant of these gifts to the extent that they show no interest in claiming them. Some even believe that there is not enough for everyone, while the scripture made it very clear that the manifestation of the spirit is given to everyone to profit from it, the disclosure of it is available to everyone, and you can have it on display if you like.

The gifts of the spirit as admirable as they are, not many believer are making any effort to claim them, while at the same time our churches could do well having them, as it could well be that we would attract more visitors to our local church, and ultimately win some to Christ. I trust that with this thought in print, it will attract some interest.

Chapter 8

CHRISTIAN IN THE LOCAL CHURCH

Light is good and pleasant, it is more desirable than darkness. Jesus told his disciples that as long as he was in the world he would be the light of the world, John 9:5, His followers should also be the light of the world Matt 5:14, 16.

Jesus uses the word light because he knows the importance of the light and that people need light to see where they are going especially at night, if there is no light, people will stumble in the darkness and will not be able to find their way out easily.

Christians are the spiritual light of the world regardless of how dim or how bright their lights are, it is better to have a small candle lit in the darkest condition, than to have no light at all. But it is even worse if you have a small candle and hide it, failing to light it so as to give light to all in the house and for helping others outside to see their way out of the darkness. Your candle will be of no value to you or others around you if you fail to light it and hold it for others to see.

This likeness is typical of many people who operate under the name of Christianity. If the inhabitants of the community wherein people operate are not shown, that they are in darkness by the light of Christians in it, they are at liberty to blame the Christian without being criticised as sceptical. Bad attitudes among Christians, carries serious consequences for the non-believer, and such consequences involve hell and everlasting punishment. This may sound drastic but a reality nonetheless.

A Christian's life and the way they live it, among themselves in the community says much to the non-believer by way of example, and the existence of God. Christian's lifestyle should reflect the sincerity behind their Christianity. The disciples were first called Christians at Antioch because of their love and unity for each other which they shared among themselves. This mutual love is important because it is evidence of the relationship between them and Christ.

We cannot love those we do not see and hate those we see, it will be very difficult. We cannot hate our brothers and love God who we cannot see, at the same time this is illogical, love is not what we say but what we do.

The good Samaritan showed love in the deed that he did. It is a fact that there are many people who are called Christians but very difficult to love, this is where genuine love excels. Genuine love comes from God; his children should be endowed with the same love, anything short of that in a person, is not the child of God. God's love was demonstrated in Jesus dying under excruciating pains not for himself but for us. The hymn writer says "I wonder what he saw in me to suffer such deep agony...." Although Jesus knew who his enemies were and who did what to him, he prayed "Father forgive them for they know not what they do".

We must therefore be able to excel the righteousness of the scribes and Pharisees in order to be sincerely qualified as children of God. They seem to be able to hate, kill and love at the same time. Jesus says that if you love those who love you what is so great about that? Are you expecting to get a reward for that? Anyone can love the people who love and speak nice things about them, but it takes the love of God in the heart to love your enemy and to pray for those who persecute you.

People believe in God when they see godly deeds done by those who profess godliness. When we give wrong signals to the non-believer, we are confusing them as well as sending them to hell at the same time. We may wonder why more people do not attend the church, the reason is simple, we fail to prove to them that what we say about God is true.

CHRISTIAN IN THE LOCAL CHURCH

Christians must be shining lights wherever they are because the world is in darkness, and the darkness is getting darker each day, evidence of this is everywhere; children have become almost unmanageable, violence happening everywhere, at home, at school and on the streets of the community and law enforcing agencies are not taking it serious.

All this is happening because parents who used to be role models to their children, teaching them the difference between right and wrong, have themselves become very ungodly. Apostasy is spreading like wild fire, all these things are the fulfilment of scriptures.

In spite of these blatant ungodly attitudes, the church of God still fail to declare where it stands regarding morality and God's righteousness; instead even the elders of society, including those in the church are involved in abnormal and immoral behaviour, that they use to condemn as immorality.

If you know the difference between right and wrong, light and darkness, stay faithful to God wherever you are, regardless of who is doing what all around you, remember that you are the light of the world, so remain as such, holding your small candle as high as you possibly can, you may not be able to save everyone, but someone somewhere in darkness you may rescue and save from destruction, all you have to do is let your little light always shine.

CHRISTIAN DEVELOPMENT AND MATURATION

Christians have a special role to play within the community, and the community is expecting the Christian to play that role well. The spiritual wellbeing of the community is the Christian's responsibility; both morally and spiritually. This means that to play his spiritual role well the Christian must always be a pattern of example, taking into consideration that people have him under constant scrutiny whether he or she is aware of it or not.

This is not an easy task because the Christian is a human being with human tendencies like any other, but this is where the dividing line between the Christian and the non-Christian is drawn. To be a spiritual pattern of example requires something superhuman, it requires the spirit of God in the life, and to get the spirit of God in the life one must be changed, this is what conversion means.

When one is converted old habits and attitudes are mortified, the flesh no more dominates, it is in subjection to the spirit of God that is living inside. The spirit is now in control and will always give a nudge when something needs careful consideration before commitment. A conscious Christian will be aware of the spirit's nudges and will not ignore them because to do so is at his peril.

A Christian in the community is of very high value even if the people in the community do not say so. Most people in the community respects him not just for what he says, people also evaluates what the

CHRISTIAN IN THE LOCAL CHURCH

Christian says as well as what they do. They do not read the bible today as they use to do when I was a lad growing up and going to Sunday school, they critically scrutinise the Christians attitude and behaviours, and they have all right to do so, because the Christians are ambassadors of Christ and should live up to their reputation, and they have a fairly accurate rating of him or her, and that is the criteria on which they measure and judge the status of the Christian in their community, (think about this).

The good Samaritan was called good because of what he did not what he said; he interrupted his journey, attended to a man who was in dire need of help, he administered to the man's needs, took him to the safety and the comfort of the hotel, paid for the service and promised to pay more if needs be. On the other hand, two people who were expected to do what the Samaritan did, but passed the wounded stranger as far as they could, showing no bowels of compassion or human kindness.

Jesus asked his disciples which of the three individuals were a neighbour to the man in dire need. Any one with common sense and human compassion should identify the Samaritan as the neighbour of the victim.

Light is good but only when it shines, salt is good only if it contain saltiness. A Christian is both the light of the world and the salt of the earth, if these values are not dispensed in the community where he or she lives, their living is in vain Matt. 5:13-16.

Christians must endeavour to shine their light wherever there is darkness, and since it is getting darker as midnight draws near, greater endeavour should be made by all Christians to shine their light in the darkness that the devil is causing all around us.

Is it our responsibility how many souls will suffer and die in hellish wars and strife that is going on all over the world? We have a moral responsibility to help those who are in darkness to escape God's judgement which is inevitable, by shining our lights for them to see their way out into the safety we know exist only in God.

In closing this chapter I would like to enclose a few ideas as to how to make your local church attractive to visitors in the community.

1.   Sharing responsibility – in John's gospel chapter 15, Jesus declares himself as the Vine and his father as the Gardener or cultivator and that his followers are the branches of the vine and he being a responsible person he carried out the necessary pruning and purging in order to secure a good harvest, a teamwork between Father and Son.

The branches responsibility (verse 4-5) Abiding in the vine meaning to cooperate with the Vine as without the Vine the branches cannot survive.

2.   Paul quoted in 1 Cor. 3:6 that he has done the planting and another person waters the plant, and

in verse 7 God gave the increase. That's sharing responsibility, and in verse 8 he declares that all together we are labourers together with God.

When members of the local church worked together, what is accomplished by the team is credited to the effort of the entire teamwork, further on in the same 1 Cor. 3 we read where it was Paul that laid the foundation of the building and others built there on and that care should be taken when you are building on other people's foundation, this warning should be heeded by all of us labouring together in God's church. The work we have done will be tested, if we build contrary to the purpose of God's will we will suffer loss, but if we endeavour to do the things He directs us to do we will be rewarded for being obedient to Him. 1 Cor. 3:12-14

If there is a time in the history of the church that Christians need to stand together to promote unity among believers this is the time. We in the western world, has never have it so good economically making it so attractive to do everything other than serving God and trusting Him to direct us in the right way to go.

This is a time in the history of the church when Christians in these parts of the world are watering down the standard of holiness, to the extent that when one takes a stand to uphold righteousness you are looked upon as being sick in the head, and church leaders are limiting the times of worship saying they are making it easier in order to get more people to attend church, not realising that it is the trick of the devil trying to weaken the church. It's no wonder that some of the churches in our community only have one meeting on Sundays and nothing more for the week except club meetings.

In chapter 7 I wrote about Spirit filled believers, by that I mean Holy Spirit filled people who have a passion in their soul to worship and serve God at any cost, people with a burning desire and a mind to please God. As I write this book I believe that there are still a few of such people in our world today, who are endeavouring to do their utmost to keep the lamp of God burning in the House of God, and ultimately in our community, and are continually praying to God to raise up Christians in our churches and communities to join forces with us, so that we will make a difference. May the Holy Spirit fire of God burn in us, until people in our community see what it is doing to us, and I am sure if they are able to see the signs and wonders that characterised the Christians of the early church, they at least will have to say that of a truth God is with us.

The Lord has put this in my heart that there are thousands of people in this country in whose heart there is a burning desire and a passion for this awakening, and are praying to God for this to come to pass.

This kind of a passion for God's intervention comes

at times when the people of God find themselves helpless, and need a change in their circumstances in relation to Holiness and Righteousness, which it takes to worship God.

It is my prayer that Christians everywhere will join forces together in prayer for a great revival in our country and our world. It is the responsibility of Christians to work together to make our churches strong under God and with His guidance, let us all do our part with a willing mind.

Chapter 9

CHRISTIAN STEWARDSHIP

A steward is responsible for his master's estate both in his master's presence as well as in his absence. He is expected to give his best to his master's service because he will have to give an account to him about what he did or did not do regarding the well being of the estate on a whole. A steward's responsibility is to prove his worth in order to justify the reward they agreed on before the employment starts. He is a very important person in his master's service and he is expected to encourage others, to perform their own role well to justify their reward, and to encourage them to get satisfaction from what they do for the master.

A Christian steward is no different from the secular steward except that his master is the Lord Jesus Christ, making the service spiritual. In other words, the spiritual steward under the Lordship of Jesus Christ and the Holy Spirit's direction, work together to convert people from a sinner to a saint.

This makes the steward a very important person in the community, where he serves as a mediator between the people of the community and God. The spiritual steward operates under the influence of the Holy Spirit, he is exempted from seeking academic qualification which the secular steward most certainly needs to have to be qualified for the post.

However, inasmuch as the spiritual steward is not dependent on academic qualification, that does not prevent him from seeking to be qualified academically, as knowledge is important for all persons and people, hence academic qualification should be earnestly sought after where possible, but the Christians who are not fortunate to have it, should not use that as an excuse for not making an effort to be a steward for God, because the greatest qualifier is the Holy Spirit and if you have Him that's more than enough for any task.

The spiritual steward's role is to get peoples prime interest away from materialistic attainment, which is decadent and get them to concentrate on the spiritual blessings, which far outweigh materialistic attainment. Materialism can only satisfy the body but spiritual blessings are for the soul that cannot die.

The spiritual stewards dealing is with people who want to enter the kingdom of God and heaven, spiritual stewards must seriously consider the

CHRISTIAN DEVELOPMENT AND MATURATION

spiritual task he or she has enrolled for, and realise that from the beginning the extent of the sacrifice they have to make.

To become an effective and trustworthy steward, the only credential needed is to be born again. This is absolutely necessary because although there are many people operating as a spiritual steward, they were not born again, although they are teaching and preaching the born again message. Those people are like Necodemus who although he was a teacher of Jewish religion, he was not even aware of what Jesus meant, when he told him that to see the kingdom of heaven he must be born again.

However, he was honest enough to seek advice when he heard about it, from someone he believes was sent from God to make the world aware of the kingdom of God and of heaven, what he was not sure about was how to enter either of them.

The potential stewards must first be honest regarding their spiritual well being, and must be willing to seek advice on how to get adjusted to their holy lives. There are many people who are very active in and around the church, but they have never been converted, and because they are not converted, they are not qualified to be God's steward, preparing God's people for the kingdom of God and heaven.

The office of a spiritual steward is different in many ways from the literal one; his employer is also different and is expected to be quite a different type of person than an ordinary steward. The main area where the difference lies, is in the behaviour, also the reward and the rate at which the reward is given.

The literal steward contracts out to his employer his physical service for a literal salary, which he gets weekly, quarterly, annually or otherwise, if he becomes dissatisfied with his employer he can resign and seek employment elsewhere doing something quite different for more or less money. He is in the job for the wages or salary they decide on at the beginning.

The spiritual steward's employment is quite different; his employment is to do the same job for life, his employment does not change, neither his salary, regardless of how long he is in the employment, and the intensity of the labour. If he leaves he cannot be re-employed by anyone else, but his job is still there waiting for him if he did return.

To the natural person this type of employment is not attractive or feasible, where one must wait to get to heaven before one gets the reward. His stewardship and reward must be received here and now, he is not interested in souls for hire or the afterlife, he wants his pay now, the pay to be received is for people who are walking in faith and working for faith, the reward is for people who live by faith. To that person many years ago Jesus made the following two statements; "*for what profit is there to a man if he gains the whole world and loose his soul*" or "*what can a man give in exchange for his soul?*" (Matt. 16:26) "*But seek ye first the kingdom of God and his righteousness and all these things shall be added unto you.*" (Matt. 6:33).

One's priority in matter of this kind determines the answer one gives to those questions. If a person's ultimate outlook in life is to become materially rich, little or no emphasis will be placed on the spiritual investment. However, if one's ultimate objective is to be eternally rewarded for his earthly stewardship in the service of God, that person will make sure that at all times, his or her reward in heaven is secured.

Who then is a spiritual steward and what is his or her role in this life? At the beginning of this chapter I tried to portray a typical steward and the characteristics of a good one in a typical material setting, and now I am going to try and paint a more vivid picture in a specific spiritual setting, which is what this book is all about.

One of Jesus' ways of making people aware of heavenly things is to say things proverbially, the following parables were given when he wanted to describe the kingdom of heaven in comparison to the kingdom of this world; "*for the kingdom of heaven is like a landowner who went out early in the morning to hire men to work in his vineyard. He agreed to pay them one denarius for the day,* (this is the equivalent of

10 English pence at today's value) *then sent them into his vineyard"...... "he went out again about the sixth hour and the ninth hour and did the same, about the eleventh hour, he went out and found others standing around, he asked them 'why have you been standing here all day long doing nothing', 'because no one has hired us' they answered. He said to them you also go and work in my vineyard. When the evening came, the owner of the vineyard said to the steward, 'call the workers and pay them their wages, beginning with the last one hired, and then going on to the first'. The workers who were hired about the eleventh hour came and each received a denarius. Then those who were hired first, expecting to receive more, but each one of them received a denarius. When they received it they began to grumble against the landowner; 'these men who were hired last worked only one hour and you have made them equal to us who have borne the burden of the work and the heat of the day, but he answered one of them 'friend I am not being unfair to you, take your pay and go your way I have the right to do what I want with my own money, or are you envious because I am generous" Matt. 20:1-16.*

"Again the kingdom of heaven will be like a man going on a journey, and before he left, calls his servants and entrusted his property to them. To one he gave five talents, to another two talents and to another one talent, each according to his ability. Then he went on his journey. The man who receives

five talents went at once and put his money to work and gained five more talents. The one with the two talents gained two more, but the man who had received the one talent went off and dug a hole in the ground and hid his master's money.

After a long time, the master of the servants returned and settled accounts with them. The man who had received five talents brought another five talents. 'Master he said, you entrusted me with five talents, see I have gained five more'. His master replied, 'well done good and faithful servant, you have been faithful with a few things; I will put you in charge of many things, come and share your master's happiness.

The man with the two talents also came. 'Master he said, you entrusted me with two talents, see I have gained two more. His master replied, 'well done good and faithful servant, you have been faithful with a few things; I will put you in charge of many things, come and share your master's happiness.

Then the man who had received one talent came. 'Master I knew that you are a hard man, harvesting where you have not sown and gathering where you have not scattered seeds, so I was afraid and I went out and hid your money in the ground, see here is what belongs to you'. His master replied, 'you wicked and lazy servant, you knew I harvest where I have not scattered seeds, well then you should have put my money on deposit with the bankers, so that when

I returned I should have received back with interest. Take the talent from him and give it to the one who has the ten talents….." Matt. 25:14-30.

The spiritual steward must therefore be both thrifty and spiritual. Thrifty in matters of honest numerical gain, and spiritually orientated regarding the standard of holiness set by God as the criteria for entering into the kingdom of heaven.

Like a father to a son the apostle Paul was quite firm in his warning to Timothy; *"But mark this he said, there will be terrible times in the last days, people will be lovers of themselves, lovers of money, boastful, proud, abusive, disobedient to their parents, ungrateful, unholy, without natural love, unforgiving, rash, conceited, lovers of pleasure rather than lovers of God, having a form or godliness but denying it's power. Have nothing to do with them"* Paul said. 2 Tim. 3:1-5

This is typical of many people in the Christian environment today; they twist the word of God to suit their own carnal outlook and try to justify themselves doing wrong things, in this way they deceive themselves and others like them, but together they eventually bring onto themselves swift damnation.

The spiritual steward is empowered by God to administer divine righteousness, and to live holy so that others under him will have him as an example, in matters of holiness as he follows Christ.

Moses was an excellent leader and his leadership

was of the kind that left on record an excellent example in matters of wisdom and humbleness, but he was not endowed with intellectual powers, where that was needed God provided Aaron. God will always provide his stewards with all they need for the job at hand. Humbleness is therefore the most important attributes of a good steward. I have been a pastor for many years and I call upon all sincere pastors or spiritual leaders, who I know will agree with me when I say that the church is not an easy place to be employed as a steward, but as long as you are called by God, he will give the wherewithal to serve and survive to the end.

By stooping down and washing the disciple's feet, Jesus was showing his disciples what it meant to be humble. *"If I being your Lord and master have washed your feet, then you too are to wash one another's feet" he said.* This is how leaders should act because Jesus showed how it should be done; he bent very low in order to washed his disciple's feet although he was their Lord and master, he did it with the attitude of a servant and not as their Lord.

A good steward is one who leads by example providing sincere service to his Lord and Saviour. Sincere stewards of Christ are those who show themselves faithful in their duty and responsibility, as they seek to dispense the ingredients and principles of life to others outside of Christ, and make sure that they follow the teachings that leads to eternal life.

Spiritual stewards should be God's role models of good deeds, showing God's righteousness to the world. They must be absolutely sincere, as God's representatives in this extremely sinful world, we must present the gospel to them with the same fervour as Jesus told it. Jesus presented the gospel in a simple but firm and consistent manner; his stewards should do likewise; add nothing nor take away nothing. Unfortunately the number one problem of society today is, the insincerity of those who claim to be Christ's representatives, some are dishonest and untruthful. Spiritual stewards should be sincere, honest and true, instead of being caught up with the glut for money and popularity, an attitude God's steward should never be found guilty of.

The day of Pentecost is most significant where the history of the church of Jesus Christ is concerned, because it was on that day the church was launched by the Holy Spirit. Having launched the church, it is he who must continue his work perfecting the saints the way he was sent to do. The stewards of the church of God must therefore be spirit filled as was the disciples on the day of Pentecost, they were perpetually possessed and as a result over three thousand souls were converted after a few hours preaching and glorifying God.

This is the only way the Holy Spirit will be able to complete the work he has started, if we work with him and not him with us. God's stewards are supposed to operate under the influence of the Holy Spirit and depend on his anointing at all times to carry out their duties effectively. Ironically, because of man's dependency on education and technology, rather than on the spirit of God, people can make impact on others by the intellectual route, which is sometimes difficult to differentiate, between the person speaking under the influence of the Holy Spirit and one speaking as an orator. This is a very distinctive point for justifying the saying that there is a spiritual decline and apostasy today, but in spite of all this I am sure that the standard of righteousness is still the same as it was on the day of Pentecost and anyone who fall short of building on the foundation the Holy Spirit laid is building on wood, hay and stubble.

I would like to conclude this chapter and this book by referring to two or three individuals, who I strongly believe, I can use to justify my concept as role models for spiritual excellence today in 2006, I have listened to many bishops, overseers, pastors and others with grand ecclesiastical titles, many of whom I am not hesitant to say are not worthy of the title they hold. I am not saying that the individuals I am going to name are perfect, but I have cause to believe they have made themselves objects of credible spiritual excellence.

The evangelist Billy Graham, as far as I am aware is a most prolific and dedicated minister of

CHRISTIAN STEWARDSHIP

the gospel of Jesus Christ since 1939. There is hardly anywhere in the world where people have never heard him or heard of him, and what they hear is all good; spiritually, morally and otherwise. Billy Graham's life and service to God since 1939 is a pattern of example, and I am proud to associate myself with his depth of commitment. I believe that he had many temptations to go off on other directions like many of us have, but like many others who have committed themselves wholly to the service of Jesus Christ, would rather suffer and remain faithful in Christ's service rather than to go the way of the filthy lucre-seekers, and cause the name of Jesus to be desecrated.

Theological titles are not an important element of the standards of holiness, some people would like to argue in favour of that, but the life giving words of the gospel spoken in sincerity is life itself, theological excellence of speech motivates the brain, but the sincere word of the gospel cleanses the heart, and sets the whole person free. My brother Billy could have become the president of the United States of America with much military power and other power at his command I am told but that would not guarantee him or anyone else a place in the kingdom of God, but like the potential leader of Egypt, and the great leader of Israel, Moses would rather to suffer affliction with the people of God than to dwell in sin's pleasure for a short period.

CHRISTIAN DEVELOPMENT AND MATURATION

Another of my nominee for the title of God's role model is my sister Gladys May Russell. To me and to almost the entire population of over three million of the island of Jamaica, she was like a saint and an example of good deeds. She wore many hats during her short life of 67 years; she was a soldier and private secretary to the chiefs of staff in the Jamaica Defence Force (J.D.F.), a civil servant in some sector of government, a secretary in the local church for over 30 years, an island-wide community worker, and a helper to all in need with whom she happened to meet. She was to them like Dorcas of the bible who when she died, many tears of sorrow was shed.

My sister's departure left many of those among whom she lived in the local community, as well as in the civil service to mourn deeply. Her life was of admirable service to her Lord and saviour and her fellowmen. The various departments wherein she faithfully served over the years, were represented at her funeral on Sunday 25th September 2005. Several prominent heads of the departments where she worked paid tributes beyond those of patronising attestations.

This was for me profound evidence of a life that has impacted me and many people, who made the sacrifice to attend her funeral, to attest my choice of nominating her as one of my favourite role model of spiritual excellence.

CHRISTIAN STEWARDSHIP

At the beginning of this book, I told you that I was not exposed to literacy at the time when I should, and as a result I was socially and intellectually handicapped until I was nearly forty years of age. At that age, I was already living in an industrially developed country instead of the under developed one I left in Jamaica. My entire social and spiritual outlook has now changed and I am seeing life from a different perspective. I also told you that although I am now at the summit of the mountain of life, I am persuaded that God has called me from a life of obscurity and has established me, so that I could become the spiritual role model that many people say that I am to them.

Now I am looking way back into the past and I am sure of a reward for service rendered to God on behalf of my fellowmen, I know that the process of maturation, which I have almost completed will be left on record for others to attest on my behalf as a model of righteousness, at least I tried and God has helped me.

To be God's role model does not come by wishful thinking, it comes by willingness to follow the leading of the Holy Spirit at all times. One must have the desire to follow in obedience where the Spirit leads and do what he say, then seek to fulfil it, not many desires, just one. David said *"one thing I desired of the Lord, that will I seek after"* Psalm 27:4, the desire is the urge one has to get or do something,

CHRISTIAN DEVELOPMENT AND MATURATION

once it is there the person always seeks to fulfil it.

A steward's desire should always be to please his master, the reward should not be the foremost reason why he serves. Pleasing his master puts him in good stead of a reward over and above that he is aware of.

When the apostle Paul mentioned that eyes have not seen nor has it entered into the hearts of men the things God has prepared for those who loved him, he hinted on the enormity of the reward in store for faithful servants of God, he went on to say that the reward is not for him only but for all who are looking for and are prepared for the master's return. He concluded by saying "I have fought a good fight, I have finished my course and I have kept the faith, henceforth is laid up for me a crown of righteousness that the Lord the righteous judge shall give not to me only but to all those who love him and look for his return." 2 Tim 4:7-8, "**Praise the Lord**".

ACKNOWLEDGEMENT

I am greatly indebted to a good friend and colleague in the ministry Pastor Albert Thomas, who I believed God has sent to help me to prepare the manuscript for this book, which I wanted to write for many years. Several friends and relatives with whom I shared my dream, encouraged me to follow my dream, but no one has ever offered me any meaningful help until this man came along, hence I see him as the one who gave me the courage to make a start, I express my sincere gratitude to him.

I also thank members of my family who played some active part; a special thanks to my wife Elfreda who stood fearlessly with me during some very strenuous times of my ministry in her effort to hold things together in tough times, as a faithful wife and loving mother, God bless her. I thank Martin for getting books from the library on how to write books, which I found very useful. Thank you Martin. Thanks also to my daughter Gwen and her husband Vince who continually urged me to get on, whenever they didn't hear me saying anything about it. Many thanks to Maureen and Yvette my daughters, between them they made their contributions in helping to

CHRISTIAN DEVELOPMENT AND MATURATION

type some part of the manuscript as well as helping to pay some of the bills. Many thanks to all of you who helped me in one way or another.

The blessings that this book will bring to those who read it, those of you who made your contribution small or great, God will bless you for your efforts. Thanks also to my many friends and brethren who prayed and asked God's direction and council in writing this book.

To all of you who made your contribution in making this book possible, some of you preferred to remain anonymous being assured that whatever one does, to promote the cause of God, will never go unrewarded, even if their names are not mentioned. God bless you all.